21 Fun Songs to Teach French Phonics

Sing and Dance your Way to Perfect Pronunciation

Catherine Cantin and Laura Maddock

We hope you and your pupils enjoy using the songs and ideas in this book. Brilliant Publications publishes many other books to help teach MFL in primary schools. To find out more details on all of our titles, including those listed below, please go to our website: www.brilliantpublications.co.uk.

100+ Fun Ideas for Practising Modern Foreign Languages in the Primary Classroom	978-1-903853-98-6
100+ Fun Ideas for Teaching French Across the Curriculum	978-1-905780-79-2
12 Petites Pièces à Jouer	978-1-905780-77-8
Bonne Idée	978-1-905780-62-4
C'est Français	978-1-903853-02-3
Chantez Plus Fort	978-1-903853-37-5
French Festivals and Traditions	978-1-905780-44-0
French is Fun at Key Stage 1	978-0-85747-830-6
French Pen Pals Made Easy	978-1-905780-10-5
French Speaking Activities	978-1-905780-66-2
Hexagonie, Part 1	978-1-905780-59-4
Hexagonie, Part 2	978-1-905780-18-1
J'aime Chanter	978-1-905780-11-2
J'aime Parler	978-1-905780-12-9
Jouons Tous Ensemble	978-1-903853-81-8
Learn French through Raps	978-0-85747-691-3
Learn French with Luc et Sophie, 1ère Partie Starter Pack, Years 3–4	978-1-78317-343-4
Learn French with Luc et Sophie, 2ème Partie Starter Pack, Years 5–6	978-1-78317-344-0
Loto Français	978-1-905780-45-7
More Fun Ideas for Advancing Modern Foreign Languages in the Primary Classroom	978-1-905780-72-3
Petites Étoiles	978-0-85747-632-6
Physical French Phonics	978-0-85747-501-5
Unforgettable French	978-1-78317-093-7

Published by Brilliant Publications Limited
Unit 10
Sparrow Hall Farm
Edlesborough
Dunstable
Bedfordshire
LU6 2ES, UK

www.brilliantpublications.co.uk

The name Brilliant Publications and the logo are registered trademarks.

Written by Catherine Cantin and Laura Maddock
Illustrated by Gaynor Berry
Designed by Brilliant Publications Limited
Videos produced by Hart McLeod Limited
Songs written and sung by Catherine Cantin and composed and produced by Laura Maddock

© Brilliant Publications Limited 2021

ISBN: 978-0-85747-849-8
(this book is sold as a set with a USB stick; the book and USB stick are not available separately)

First printed and published in the UK in 2021.
10 9 8 7 6 5 4 3 2 1

The right of Catherine Cantin and Laura Maddock to be identified as the authors of this work has been asserted by them in accordance with the Copyright, Designs and Patents Act 1988.

Pages 14–57 may be photocopied by individual teachers acting on behalf of the purchasing institution for classroom use only, without permission from the publisher or declaration to the Copyright Licensing Agency or Publishers' Licensing Services. The materials may not be reproduced in any other form or for any other purpose without the prior permission of the publisher.

Contents

	page
About the authors	4
Introduction	5
How to use this resource	6
Phonics focus for each song	8
Teaching ideas	10

Songs

1. Il y a quelqu'**un** ?	Is anybody there?	14
2. Mon cachal**ot**	My whale	16
3. Mon petit l**ou**p	My little wolf	18
4. Une araig**n**ée dans ma baig**n**oire	A spider in my bathtub	20
5. L**u**l**u** la tort**u**e	Lulu the turtle	22
6. Le rock 'n' roll du coch**on**	The piggy rock 'n' roll	24
7. Mon ami Juli**en**	My friend Julien	26
8. Le **ch**at en **ch**ocolat	The chocolate cat	28
9. Il y a une petite bê**t**e	There is a little bug	30
10. Petit **en**fa**n**t	Little child	32
11. François le **s**erpent	François the snake	34
12. **Ga**ston le **go**rille	Gaston the gorilla	36
13. **Gi**g**i** et **Ge**orge**s**	Gigi and George	38
14. Chl**oé et** Barnab**é**	Chloe and Barnaby	40
15. Du lund**i** au d**i**manche	From Monday to Sunday	42
16. Papy, raconte-m**oi** une hist**oi**re !	Grandpa, tell me a story	44
17. Une glace à la van**ille**	Vanilla ice cream	46
18. Le rap du **h**érisson	The hedgehog rap	48
19. Q**u**'est-ce q**u**e ... ?	What ...?	50
20. Troi**s** oi**s**eaux	Three birds	52
21. Le petit canard **C**oin-**c**oin	Quack-quack the little duck	54

French phonics progress chart: key graphemes	56
French phonics progress chart: all graphemes used in songs	57
English translations of songs	58
Worksheet answers	63

The bold letters in each song title indicate the phonic focus.
For example: 'Mon petit l**ou**p' focuses on the French phonic sound '**ou**'.

About the authors

Catherine Cantin

Catherine obtained her First-Class Honours degree in English and French from the University of Warwick in 2003. She then moved to Paris where she worked for five years, before carrying out her PGCE in Modern Foreign Languages at the University of Exeter.

After obtaining her PGCE, she worked for five years as a secondary teacher of French and Spanish, before taking a break to have children.

After her second child was born, she set up her own business teaching French to babies, toddlers and their parents and grandparents. Teaching French through singing and dancing was a fantastic and transformative experience, and this led to Catherine's current role teaching French to nursery and primary school children, aged 2–11 years old.

Making the most of children's natural enjoyment and enthusiasm for singing and dancing, Catherine has been able to hone her craft and create songs, poems and raps that capture the children's imagination and embed French vocabulary, phonics and grammar into their long-term memories.

Through the songs, gestures, videos and worksheets provided in this publication, Catherine hopes to pass on the flame of her passion and life-long love of learning languages.

Laura Maddock

With a childhood immersed in music, playing instruments and performance, Laura went on to gain a BA Hons at Bretton Hall, University of Leeds. Her career started by touring in the UK providing workshops in rap and break dancing, before becoming a piano and vocal coach in New York.

Laura then travelled around the world with her guitar and campervan called "Skippy"! During this time, she wrote songs and created a new technique for teaching music to pre-schoolers through story, dance and song.

After her travels Laura continued to train and work for the Technics Music Academy, Yamaha School of Music and Worcester Music Academy. Laura is now the Director of her own Music School in Worcester.

Laura's enthusiasm and love for playing music is infectious and her students have appeared on the TV, won awards at music festivals and together have raised thousands of pounds for local charities.

With Laura's international experiences of music she was able to bring different arrangements and styles to this fun and interactive French learning resource.

Introduction

Welcome to **21 Fun Songs to Teach French Phonics**! The 21 songs featured in this book have been purposefully written, each with a different French phonic focus. By using these songs and the accompanying worksheets, we guarantee a fun and interactive method to embed both French phonics and common vocabulary and phrases into your French curriculum.

Even before children are born, they are learning about sound, rhythm and language. Long before they can talk or walk, children are bathed in a world of movement and music, where they are sung to, cradled, rocked and bounced on their parents' knees in time to the beat of a nursery rhyme or lullaby. Learning language through music and movement is a very natural process to children, and we have endeavoured to emulate this process.

Once children have a basic grasp of oracy in their mother tongue, they are then taught a programme of phonics, to facilitate their ability to read and write. Sound and spelling links are the basic building blocks upon which a child's fluency is developed. We feel that it is as important, if not more so, to develop the same skills in second language acquisition.

Each of the songs is based on a different phoneme from the French language. This allows you to provide a specific phonic focus for your lesson. However, the lyrics have also been written with the primary MFL curriculum in mind, and so you will find a wealth of age-appropriate, frequently used vocabulary and phrases. The songs can therefore also be used to reinforce different topics and units of work, as well as to focus on French phonics. The songs can be used throughout Key Stages 1 and 2, and many would be appropriate for revision in Key Stage 3.

We are confident that you and your pupils will enjoy singing, dancing and moving to these catchy French songs. We hope that you will also see the benefits in their oral, writing, listening and reading skills and, above all, in their confidence and motivation to communicate in French.

How to use this resource

This resource contains 21 French songs, specially written and composed to facilitate the introduction and reinforcement of key phonic sounds at Key Stages 1 and 2. The resource will be invaluable for both specialist and non-specialist teachers of French.

The resource uses a multi-sensory approach to help pupils learn and remember the phonemes and the graphemes associated with them. Each song focuses on a particular phoneme, which is repeated frequently in the song. To help embed correct pronunciation of the phonemes, a word and image has been purposefully chosen for each one, linking to the corresponding song and, on the video, there are actions associated with each. Children should be encouraged to copy the actions in the videos.

ch   chat

On the USB stick you will find:
- Audio tracks for all 21 songs
- Instrumental versions of the songs, to enable 'karaoke' performances
- Video for each song, so that pupils can listen to the words and watch and copy the actions. This will be invaluable for non-specialist teachers

- Colour frieze of all the phonemes introduced, which can be printed out and displayed in the classroom. There are two versions: the first one has just one key grapheme for each phoneme and is designed for use with children starting to learn French; the second contains all the graphemes linked to that phoneme that are used in the associated song. It will be beneficial for use with more advanced learners. (Note: en/an are introduced together on the key grapheme chart as they are both used in the word « enfant ».)

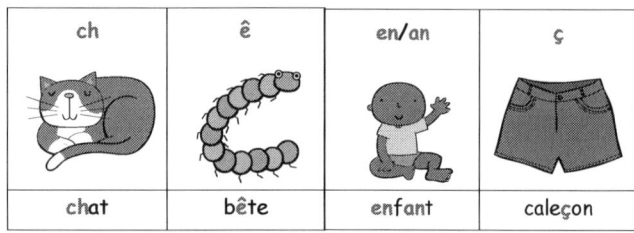   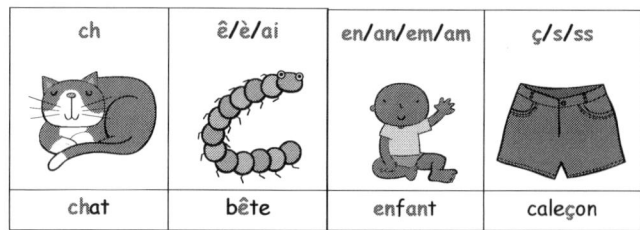

Colour frieze of key phonemes   Colour frieze of all phonemes used in the associated song

- Colour versions of the two French phonics charts. As with the frieze, there are two versions: one with just key graphemes and the other with all the graphemes used in the song associated with that phoneme. These charts can be printed out and displayed in the classroom. (If you are able to enlarge the charts to A3, this would be a bonus.)

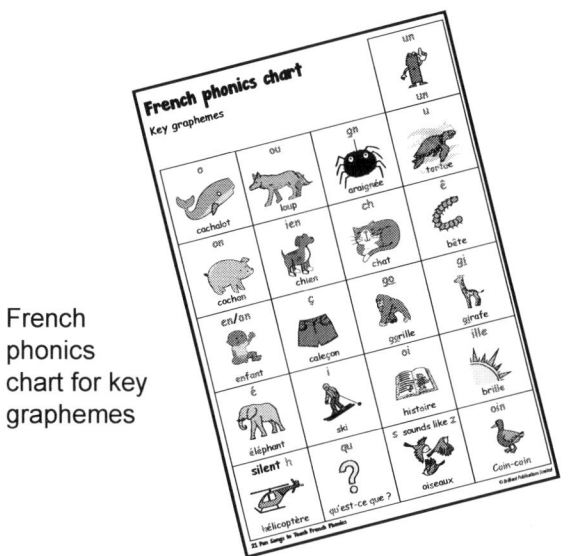

French phonics chart for key graphemes

French phonics chart for all graphemes used in the associated song

In the book you will find:
- Lyrics page for each song. This doubles up as a colouring sheet for beginners
- Worksheet for each song for use with more advanced learners
- Phonics focus for each song (pages 8–9), showing the graphemes associated with each phoneme, the song title, image and key word and other examples of the phoneme used in the song
- Teaching notes offering some additional ideas on how to exploit the songs and for possible extension work in the classroom and beyond (pages 10–13)
- French phonics progress charts (pages 56–57). These can be photocopied and stuck in children's workbooks, to allow them to colour in each phoneme as they cover it and thus chart their progress. (There are two versions: one with just the key graphemes and the second with all the graphemes used in the song associated with that phoneme)
- English translations of the songs
- Answers for the worksheets.

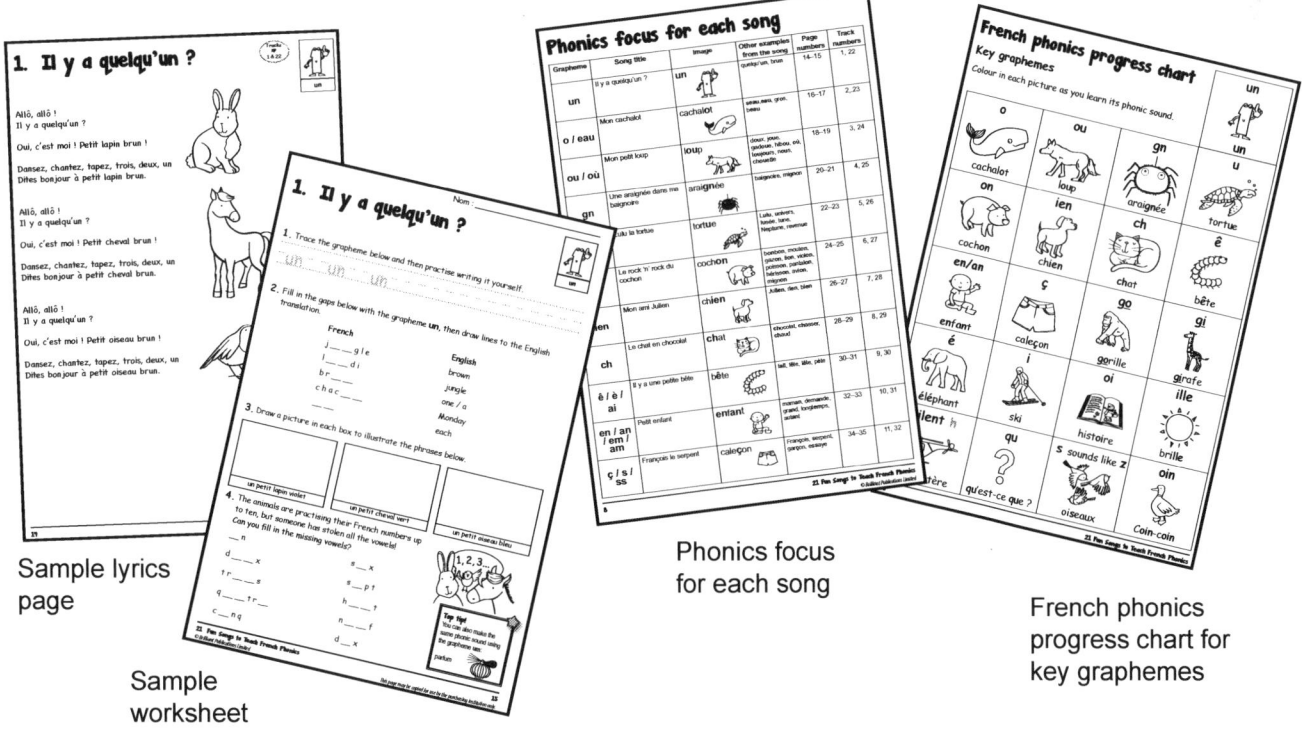

Sample lyrics page

Sample worksheet

Phonics focus for each song

French phonics progress chart for key graphemes

21 Fun Songs to Teach French Phonics

© Brilliant Publications Limited

Phonics focus for each song

Grapheme	Song title	Image	Other examples from the song	Page numbers	Track numbers
un	Il y a quelqu'un ?	un	quelqu'un, brun	14–15	1, 22
o/eau	Mon cachalot	cachalot	seau, eau, gros, beau	16–17	2, 23
ou/où	Mon petit loup	loup	où, doux, joue, gadoue, hibou, toujours, nous, chouette	18–19	3, 24
gn	Une araignée dans ma baignoire	araignée	baignoire, mignon	20–21	4, 25
u	Lulu la tortue	tortue	Lulu, univers, fusée, lune, Neptune, revenue	22–23	5, 26
on	Le rock 'n' rock du cochon	cochon	bonbon, mouton, gazon, lion, violon, poisson, pantalon, hérisson, avion, mignon	24–25	6, 27
ien	Mon ami Julien	chien	Julien, rien, bien	26–27	7, 28
ch	Le chat en chocolat	chat	chocolat, chasser, chaud	28–29	8, 29
ê/è/ai	Il y a une petite bête	bête	fait, fête, tête, pète	30–31	9, 30
en/an/em/am	Petit enfant	enfant	maman, demande, grand, longtemps, autant	32–33	10, 31
ç/s/ss	François le serpent	caleçon	François, serpent, garçon, essaye	34–35	11, 32

Grapheme	Song title	Image	Other examples from the song	Page numbers	Track numbers
ga/go/gu	Gaston le gorille	gorille	Gaston, guitare, fatigué, godasses	36–37	12, 33
gi/ge/gé/j	Gigi et Georges	girafe	Gigi, Georges, géante, jour	38–39	13, 34
é/et/er	Chloé et Barnabé	éléphant	Chloé, et, Barnabé, fée, école, vélo, préféreraient, aller, fusée, décident	40–41	14, 35
i	Du lundi au dimanche	ski	lundi, mardi, mercredi, jeudi, vendredi, samedi, dimanche	42–43	15, 36
oi	Papy, raconte-moi une histoire !	histoire	moi, froid, noir, crois, couloir, rois, bois, loi, quoi, étoile, toi	44–45	16, 37
ille	Une glace à la vanille	brille	famille, fille, vanille	46–47	17, 38
silent h	Le rap du hérisson	hélicoptère	hérisson, Hervé, hic, hoquet, hôpital, Hector, hippo, Harry, hamster, hamburgers, histoire, hip, hoorah	48–49	18, 39
qu	Qu'est-ce que ...?	qu'est-ce que	Examples from the worksheet: qui, quand, quel, est-ce que, pourquoi	50–51	19, 40
S sounds like Z	Trois oiseaux	oiseaux	fraises, raisins, cerises, bise (There are also examples of liaison in the song)	52–53	20, 41
oin	Le petit canard Coin-coin	Coin-coin	loin, foin, besoin	54–55	21, 42

21 Fun Songs to Teach French Phonics

© Brilliant Publications Limited

Teaching ideas

Here are some ideas for activities and games to support the teaching and learning of **21 Fun Songs to Teach French Phonics**.

Spot the French phonics!
Work as a class, in teams or individually.
Using the lyrics: project the grapheme(s) on to the board. Give groups a printout of the lyrics and then play the song. Whenever students hear the corresponding phoneme, they have to underline the word that it is found in. This can also be done without playing the music, with children reading the lyrics instead.

Using physical gestures: play the song and every time the pupils hear the phoneme, they raise their hand/do the action you have chosen as a class.

1. Il y a quelqu'un ?   page 14
Choose one pupil to be the 'caller' and then split the rest of the class into three groups. The caller says the line « Allô, allô? Il y a quelqu'un ? » The other three groups represent the rabbit, horse and bird. They each sing their verse and must come up with their own actions. All pupils can join in with « Chantez, dansez, tapez trois, deux, un » etc. Remember to switch the groups around so that every child gets a go at each part.

2. Mon cachalot   page 16
What else might the pupils find in their bucket? Brainstorm some vocabulary using the pupils' ideas and then reinforce the phrase: « dans mon seau il y a un/une… .» The song could then be performed replacing the word « cachalot » for one of the pupils' words instead. The concept of gender and the indefinite article could be introduced/reinforced at this point.

3. Mon petit loup   page 18
Split the class up into pairs. One pupil is the child and the other pupil is the wolf. Can they use the lyrics like a script and act out the story? If you have any very shy or reluctant pupils, they could be the owl and join in with the actions. Ask for volunteers to act out the story to the rest of the class.

4. Une araignée dans ma baignoire   page 20
Arts and craft activity: make a spider! You will need 8 pipe cleaners, 1 pompom, 2 googly eyes and some glue. You can use this activity to introduce body parts (la tête, les yeux, les pattes, etc).

5. Lulu la tortue   page 22
Can pupils imagine who Lulu may have met on Neptune? Who did she play football with? What did she eat for her picnic? Brainstorm vocabulary on the board and then ask them to draw and label a picture.

6. Le rock 'n' roll du cochon — page 24

Split the class in half. Have one half leading the singing and the other half singing the echoes. Ask for a volunteer to lead on their own and have the rest of the class echo them.

The teacher calls out an animal and the rest of the class have to do the corresponding action, e.g. « *le cochon….mange des bonbons* » (the pig is eating sweets). This could be turned into a game of *Jacques a dit* (Simon says) or you could ask for a pupil to be the teacher and call out the animals. Alternatively, the teacher does an action, e.g. eating sweets, and asks the students to call out which animal the action belongs to. In this case it would be « *le cochon* ».

Can the pupils think of any other animals that could be doing something funny or surprising? Can they draw a picture and label it? Perhaps a new version of the song could be made up using the pupils' ideas.

7. Mon ami Julien — page 26

Ask the pupils to replace the animals in the song with other animals of their choice (*dinosaure, licorne, cochon d'Inde,* etc). Use this song as an opportunity to talk about their pets using the question: « *As-tu un animal ?* » (Do you have an animal?). Pupils can respond with: « *oui, j'ai un/ une …* » or « *non, mais j'aimerais un/une …* ».

8. Le chat en chocolat — page 28

Pupils stand in a circle. Whilst singing the song, they have to pass the ball around the circle. (It can be thrown across the circle to make it harder.) If the ball is dropped, then they have to sing the song again from the start. The aim of the game is to get to the end of the song without dropping the ball. Harder than it sounds!

This song can also be used to demonstrate the French vowel sounds: a, e, i, o, u. Each of the five verses concentrates on one vowel sound:
1) *chat, chocolat, rat* (a)
2) *oeufs, heureux* (e)
3) *sourit, ami* (i)
4) *eau, chaud* (o)
5) *disparu, déçu* (u)

9. Il y a une petite bête — page 30

Sit in a circle and use a soft toy to represent the « *bête* ». Whilst singing the song one pupil walks around the circle. When it gets to the chorus (*elle danse, elle chante …,* etc) the child stops and gets the soft toy to act out singing and dancing on the head of the person he or she is stood behind. At the end of the chorus, the child who was sitting under the « *bête* » takes over, walking around the circle until the next chorus, etc. Be warned: pupils will probably also want to act out the line: « *il faudrait pas qu'elle pète !* » (let's hope it doesn't trump!)

10. Petit enfant — page 32

Practise using numbers: ask pupils to measure each other's height, and see if they can tell the rest of the class how tall they are using French numbers, e.g. *un mètre vingt*.

Who is *le/la plus grand(e) dans la classe* (the tallest in the class) and *le/la plus petit(e)* (the smallest)? The phrases « *je suis grand(e), je suis petit(e), je suis de taille moyenne* » (I am tall/short/ medium height) could be introduced/reinforced.

11. François le serpent — page 34

Ask pupils to design and label a pair of boxer shorts (or other items of clothing) for François. This could be a good opportunity to revise clothing, colours and adjective position and agreement. The pupils' designs could be displayed or cut out and hung up on a washing line in the classroom.

12. Gaston le gorille — page 36

Practising musical instruments: ask pupils to change the song lyrics so that Gaston plays other instruments. Reinforce the construction « *jouer de + instrument* »: *je joue de la guitare, je joue de la batterie, je joue du piano* … (I play guitar, I play drums, I play piano…)

13. Gigi et Georges — page 38

Ask your pupils to draw a storyboard or comic strip of Gigi and Georges.

Can the pupils think of another unlikely pair of animal friends? Ask them to draw a picture, come up with names for their animals and then write a sentence: « *X et Y sont amis* » (X and Y are friends).

14. Chloé et Barnabé — page 40

Take the pupils on a walk in a line around the corridors/classroom/gardens. The teacher gives an instruction «*en marchant* », « *en sautant* », « *en dansant* » and the pupils must continue to follow the teacher using the movement that has been given. Ask a volunteer to be the teacher and call out the instructions.

15. Du lundi au dimanche — page 42

Call out different lines from the song and pupils have to do the action to go with that line; e.g. « *mercredi, je fais du ski* » (skiing). When the pupils get good at it, just say the day of the week in French (i.e. leave out the action) and see if they can remember.

Ask a pupil to volunteer acting out an activity from the song and the rest of the class have to call out which day of the week it represents.

Ask pupils to come up with their own list of activities they would do on each day of the week. This would coincide nicely with a topic on sports and hobbies, or pupils could use dictionaries to look up the vocabulary they need.

16. Papy, raconte-moi une histoire ! — page 44

Split the class into small groups. Provide them with simple story books in French and ask them to read a page or so each to the other pupils.

The teacher draws an image on the board and the pupils have to guess which line from the song the teacher has tried to illustrate. After a couple of rounds, put the pupils into pairs and get them to repeat the activity. The person guessing must say the line in French.

17. Une glace à la vanille — page 46

Ask the pupils to design and label their own ice cream. Brainstorm the vocabulary for cherries, strawberries, nuts, chocolate chips, raspberry sauce, etc. Ask them to write a paragraph describing their ice creams (including colours and flavours). Teach them the phrase « *C'est délicieux !* » This would make a great wall display.

18. Le rap du hérisson   page 48

Split the class into four groups and assign each group a different verse from the rap. Each group must then make up their actions and act out their verse in their own way. For example, they may decide to say one line each and then all join in on the last line, or they may decide to say the whole verse in unison. The class then has a 'rap party', where each group shows the rest of the class how they have arranged their verse. This could even be made into a competition with points awarded for creativity, pronunciation, teamwork etc.

Challenge: can pupils translate the sentences they created in exercise 2 into English (on page 49)?

19. Qu'est-ce que ... ?   page 50

Working in pairs or small groups, ask pupils to change the lyrics of the song to describe other activities for today, yesterday and tomorrow. Pupils will be able to use the same tense constructions (*je* + verb conjugated in the present tense, *j'ai* + past participle, *je vais* + infinitive) and simply change the activity, and/or the person they are doing the activity with, e.g: « *je joue au rugby avec mon père* » (I play rugby with my dad). Ideas can be brainstormed on the board before pupils break off into pairs/groups. Ask for volunteers to read out their sentences to the rest of the class.

On the lyric sheet, pupils could draw lines from the pictures to the relevant verses.

20. Trois oiseaux   page 52

Use this song as an opportunity to discuss other animals and mini-beasts you might find in the garden. Which animal would the pupils like to be? Pupils could draw and label a picture, then write a sentence using a template: « *Je voudrais être… un escargot/une araignée/un écureuil* », etc.

21. Le petit canard Coin-coin   page 54

One pupil is chosen to leave the room. Another student hides a plastic duck. The pupil is called back into the room and tasked with finding the missing duck. The other pupils can help by remaining silent if the pupil is nowhere near the duck, or by saying « *coin-coin* » if they are getting closer. The pupils chanting « *coin-coin* » will get louder the closer the 'finder' gets to discovering the duck!

1. Il y a quelqu'un ?

un

Allô, allô !
Il y a quelqu'un ?

Oui, c'est moi ! Petit lapin brun !

Dansez, chantez, tapez, trois, deux, un
Dites bonjour à petit lapin brun.

Allô, allô !
Il y a quelqu'un ?

Oui, c'est moi ! Petit cheval brun !

Dansez, chantez, tapez, trois, deux, un
Dites bonjour à petit cheval brun.

Allô, allô !
Il y a quelqu'un ?

Oui, c'est moi ! Petit oiseau brun !

Dansez, chantez, tapez, trois, deux, un
Dites bonjour à petit oiseau brun.

Nom : _____

1. Il y a quelqu'un ?

un

1. Trace the grapheme below and then practise writing it yourself.

un   un   un

2. Fill in the gaps in the words below with the grapheme **un**, then draw lines between each word and its English translation.

French	English
j __ __ g l e	brown
l __ __ d i	jungle
b r __ __	one / a / an
c h a c __ __	Monday
__ __	each

3. Draw a picture in each box to illustrate the phrases below.

un petit lapin violet	un petit cheval vert	un petit oiseau bleu

4. The animals are practising their French numbers up to ten, but someone has stolen all the vowels! Can you fill in the missing vowels?

__ n   s __ x

d __ __ x   s __ p t

t r __ __ s   h __ __ t

q __ __ t r __   n __ __ f

c __ n q   d __ x

Top tip!
You can also make the same phonic sound using the grapheme **um**:

parfum

2. Mon cachalot

o/eau

J'ai un seau
Un joli seau
Dans mon seau
Il y a de l'eau.

J'ai un seau
Un joli seau
Dans mon seau
Il se cache un cachalot !

Un cachalot ?
Un cachalot !

Oooh là là, qu'il est gros !
Oooh là, là, qu'il est beau !
Mon cachalot
Plouf !

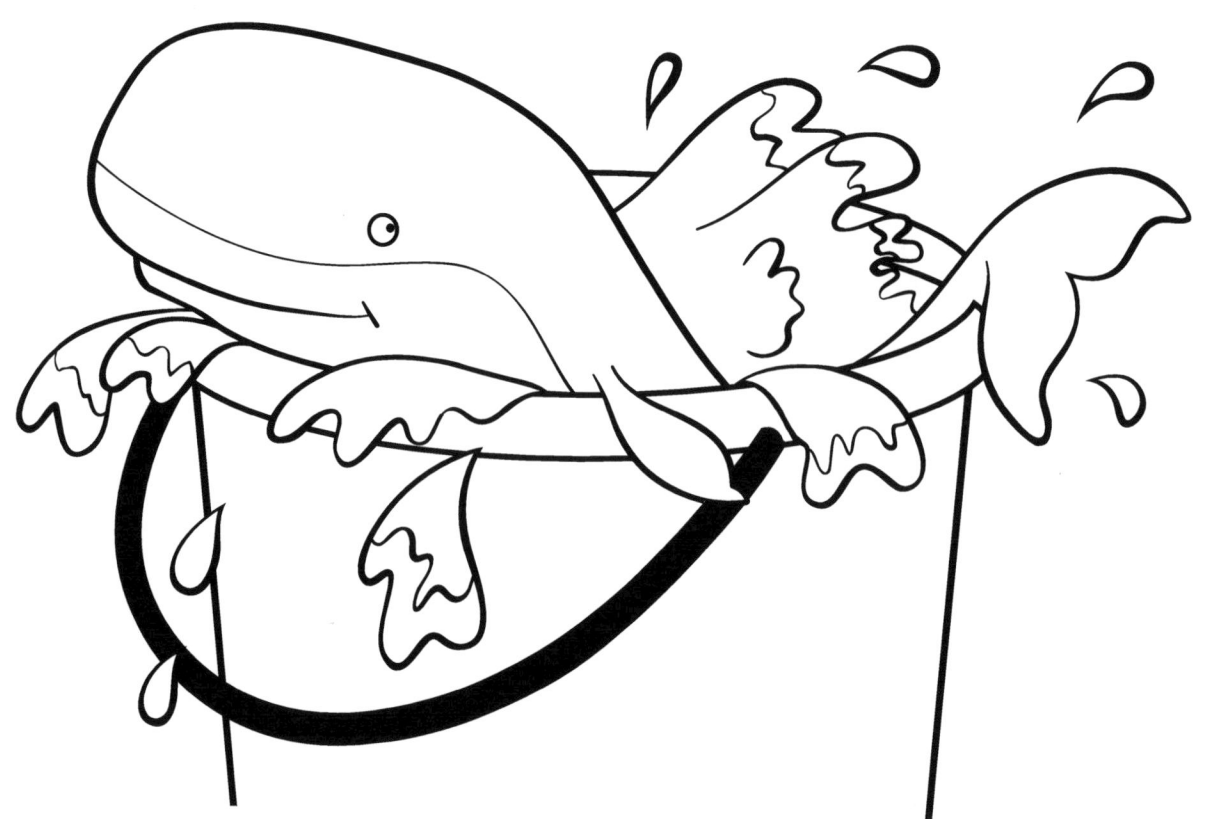

Nom : _____

2. Mon cachalot

o/eau

1. Trace the graphemes below and then practise writing them yourself.

o o o o

eau eau

2. Circle the four words below that contain the grapheme **o** and rhyme with **cachalot**.

dans   gros   gris   stylo   sac   dos   rouge   mot

3. Circle the four words below that contain the grapheme **eau** and rhyme with **cachalot**.

beurre   faux   seau   feutre   bateau   beau   taupe   chapeau

4. Rearrange the syllables in the whale's spout to make the French word for whale. Write it in the sentence below.

Dans mon seau, il y a un _____ .

5. Draw a picture of something you would like to find in your **seau**, then write a sentence about it in French. Can you add any extra details?

Dans mon seau il y a _____

_____

Top tip!
You can also make the same phonic sound using the following graphemes:
ô   hôtel (*hotel*)   au   jaune (*yellow*)

3. Mon petit loup

ou

Où es-tu, mon petit loup,
Mon petit loup, tout doux ?

Moi, je joue dans la gadoue
Avec mon ami le hibou.

Où es-tu, mon petit loup,
Mon petit loup, tout doux ?

Moi, je joue dans la gadoue
Avec mon ami le hibou.

Mon petit loup
Tu ne m'aimes plus !
Toujours avec ton hibou !

Ne sois pas bête,
Fais pas la tête,
Viens faire la fête avec nous,
Viens faire la fête avec nous !

On fait la fête ?
Chouette !

Nom : _____

3. Mon petit loup

ou

1. Trace the grapheme below and then practise writing it yourself.

ou   ou   ou

2. Draw a circle around every **ou** grapheme in the box below:

| ou | oi | au | ou | oe | ou | oo | oa | ou | uo | ou | on |
| on | ou | oi | oo | ou | uo | ou | on | oi | ou | on | om |

How many **ou** graphemes did you circle? ☐

3. Fill in the gaps in the words below with the grapheme **ou**, then draw lines between each word and the correct image.

l __ __ p   hib __ __

b __ __ les   gad __ __ e

4. Colour in the boxes below that contain words with the grapheme **ou**. Leave the boxes that don't contain words with the grapheme **ou** blank.

fourmi	souris	journal	tortue
poule	bateau	douche	boîte
amour	bonbon	soupe	route

How many boxes did you colour in? ☐

5. Imagine you are **petit loup**. What else do you play with your friend, **le hibou**? Finish off the sentence below in French. There are some ideas underneath to help you.

Je joue _____.

4. Une araignée dans ma baignoire

gn

Il y a une araignée dans ma baignoire
Elle est poilue, grande et toute noire !
Je n'ai même pas peur, non, non, non,
Avoir une amie-araignée, c'est mignon.

C'est mignon, mignon, mignon, mignon
C'est mignon, mignon, mignon, mignon.

Il y a une araignée dans ma baignoire
Elle est poilue, grande et toute noire.
Je n'ai même pas peur, non, non, non,
Avoir une amie-araignée, c'est mignon !

C'est mignon, mignon, mignon, mignon
C'est mignon, mignon, mignon, mignon.

Et toi, tu aimes les araignées ?

Nom : _____

4. Une araignée dans ma baignoire

gn

1. Trace the grapheme below and then practise writing it yourself.

gn   gn   gn

2. Circle the four words below that contain the grapheme **gn**.

montagne   plage   poignet   pigeon   cochon   mignon   baignoire

3. Practise saying the phrases below that contain words with the grapheme **gn**. Get your partner or teacher to listen to you and then tick the image when you are confident you can say the word correctly.

À la **campagne** il y a des **araignées** et des **champignons**.

Les **cygnes** volent en **ligne** vers les **montagnes**.

4. Draw **une araignée** in a **baignoire** below. Make sure your **araignée** is **poilue** (hairy), **grande** (big) and **toute noire** (black all over)!

5. Tu aimes les araignées ? (Do you like spiders?) Answer in French using phrases from the vocabulary box below.

_____

_____

_____

Vocabulary	
Oui	**Yes**
J'aime les araignées.	I like spiders.
Je n'ai pas peur des araignées.	I'm not afraid of spiders.
Non	**No**
Je n'aime pas les araignées.	I don't like spiders.
J'ai peur des araignées.	I'm afraid of spiders.

5. Lulu la tortue

Lulu la tortue
Un jour a décidé
De voyager à travers l'univers
Dans sa petite fusée.

5, 4, 3, 2, 1 – whoosh !

Elle a pique-niqué sur la lune

Elle a joué au foot sur Neptune

Et après ce voyage extraordinaire,
Tout doucement,
Tout doucement,
Tout doucement …
Elle est revenue sur la terre
Elle est revenue sur la terre.

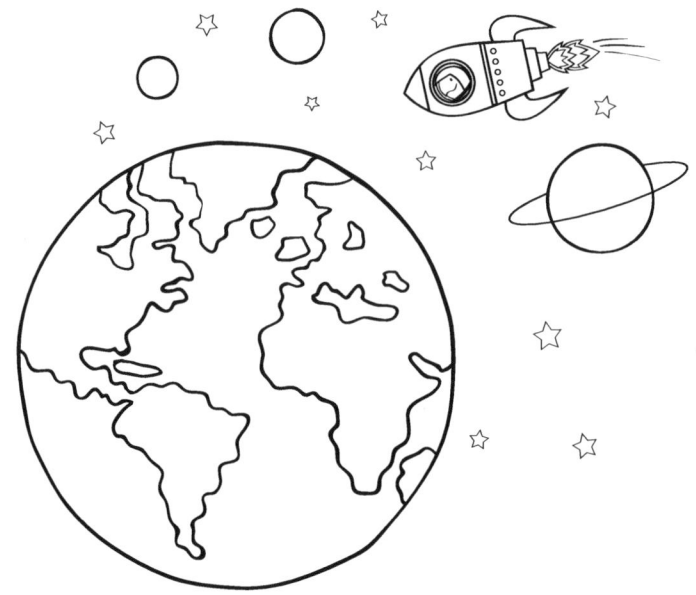

Nom : _____

5. Lulu la tortue

u

1. Trace the grapheme below and then practise writing it yourself.

u u u u

2. Draw pictures below to complete the comic strip about the adventures of **Lulu la tortue**, then read the comic strip out loud.

Lulu la tortue	un jour a decidé	de voyager à travers l'univers

| dans sa petite fusée. | 5, 4, 3, 2, 1 – whoosh ! | Elle a pique-niqué sur la lune |

tout doucement

| elle a joué au foot sur Neptune. | Et après ce voyage extraordinaire | elle est revenue sur la terre. |

21 Fun Songs to Teach French Phonics

6. Le rock 'n' roll du cochon

on

Venez, venez, on va chanter le rock 'n' roll des animaux !

Le rock 'n' roll des animaux
Le rock 'n' roll des animaux

Le cochon, le cochon, le cochon … mange des bonbons !

Le rock 'n' roll des animaux
Le rock 'n' roll des animaux

Le mouton, le mouton, le mouton … tond le gazon !

Le rock 'n' roll des animaux
Le rock 'n' roll des animaux

Le lion, le lion, le lion … joue du violon !

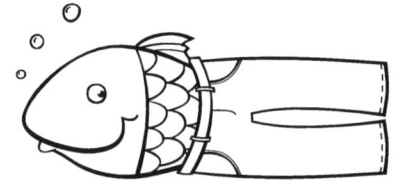

Le rock 'n' roll des animaux
Le rock 'n' roll des animaux

Le poisson, le poisson, le poisson … porte un pantalon !

Le rock 'n' roll des animaux
Le rock 'n' roll des animaux

Le hérisson, le hérisson, le hérisson … pilote un avion !

Qu'est-ce qu'ils sont mignons !

Nom : _____

6. Le rock 'n' roll du cochon

on

1. Trace the grapheme below and then practise writing it yourself.

on   on   on

2. Rearrange the letters in each animal below to spell out their name in French.

_____ _____ _____ _____ _____

3. Draw lines to match up the words with the correct images.

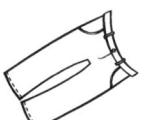

a) bonbon
b) gazon
c) violon
d) pantalon
e) avion

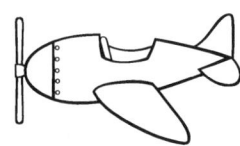

4. Draw pictures to illustrate the phrases in the boxes below:

Le cochon mange des bonbons.	Le poisson porte un pantalon.	Le hérisson pilote un avion.

Top tip!
You can also make the same phonic sound using the grapheme **om**:
  ombre (*shadow*)   **combien** (*how much*)   **bombe** (*bomb*)   **tomber** (*to fall*)

21 Fun Songs to Teach French Phonics
© Brilliant Publications Limited

7. Mon ami Julien

ien

J'ai un ami qui s'appelle Julien
Il aimerait un petit chien
Mais son père dit : non, non, non !

Ça ne sert à rien, d'avoir un petit chien
Quand tu as déjà un pingouin !

J'ai un ami qui s'appelle Julien
Il aimerait un petit chien
Mais son père dit : non, non, non !

Ça ne sert à rien, d'avoir un petit chien
Quand tu as déjà un babouin !

J'ai un ami qui s'appelle Julien
Il aimerait un petit chien
Mais son père dit : non, non, non !

Ça ne sert à rien, d'avoir un petit chien
Quand tu as déjà un requin !

Plutôt qu'un chien mon père
Pourquoi pas un petit frère ?

Finalement, mon Julien
Un petit chien, c'est très bien !

Nom : _____

7. Mon ami Julien

ien

1. Trace the grapheme below and then practise writing it yourself.

ien   ien   ien

2. Circle the four words below that contain the grapheme **ien** and rhyme with the word **Julien**.

(chat   chien   cheval   rien   rhino   bien   banane   magicien)

3. Draw pictures to illustrate the words in the boxes below:

un pingouin

un babouin

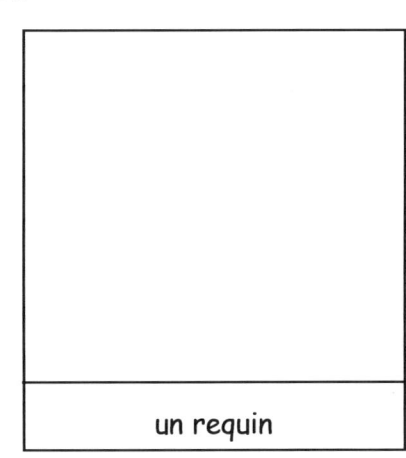
un requin

4. Choose some animals from the vocabulary box below that you would like to have, then complete the sentence. The word for 'and' in French is **et**.

J'aimerais _____

_____

_____

_____

Vocabulary			
un éléphant		une girafe	
un panda		une baleine	
un lion		une tortue	
un dauphin		une vache	
un aigle		une araignée	
un hippopotame		une souris	

21 Fun Songs to Teach French Phonics

© Brilliant Publications Limited   This page may be copied for use by the purchasing institution only.

8. Le chat en chocolat

ch

Je vois le chat, chat, chat
En chocolat, lat, lat
Qui ne veut pas, pas, pas
Chasser le rat, rat, rat !

Je vois le chat, chat, chat
En chocolat, lat, lat
Qui mange des oeufs, oeufs, oeufs
Il est heureux, reux, reux !

Je vois le chat, chat, chat
En chocolat, lat, lat
Il me sourit, rit, rit
C'est mon ami, mi, mi !

Je vois le chat, chat, chat
En chocolat, lat, lat
Il boit de l'eau, l'eau, l'eau
Il a trop chaud, chaud, chaud !

Le petit chat chat chat
En chocolat, lat lat
A disparu, ru, ru
Je suis déçu, çu, çu.

Mais non, je suis là ! Coucou !

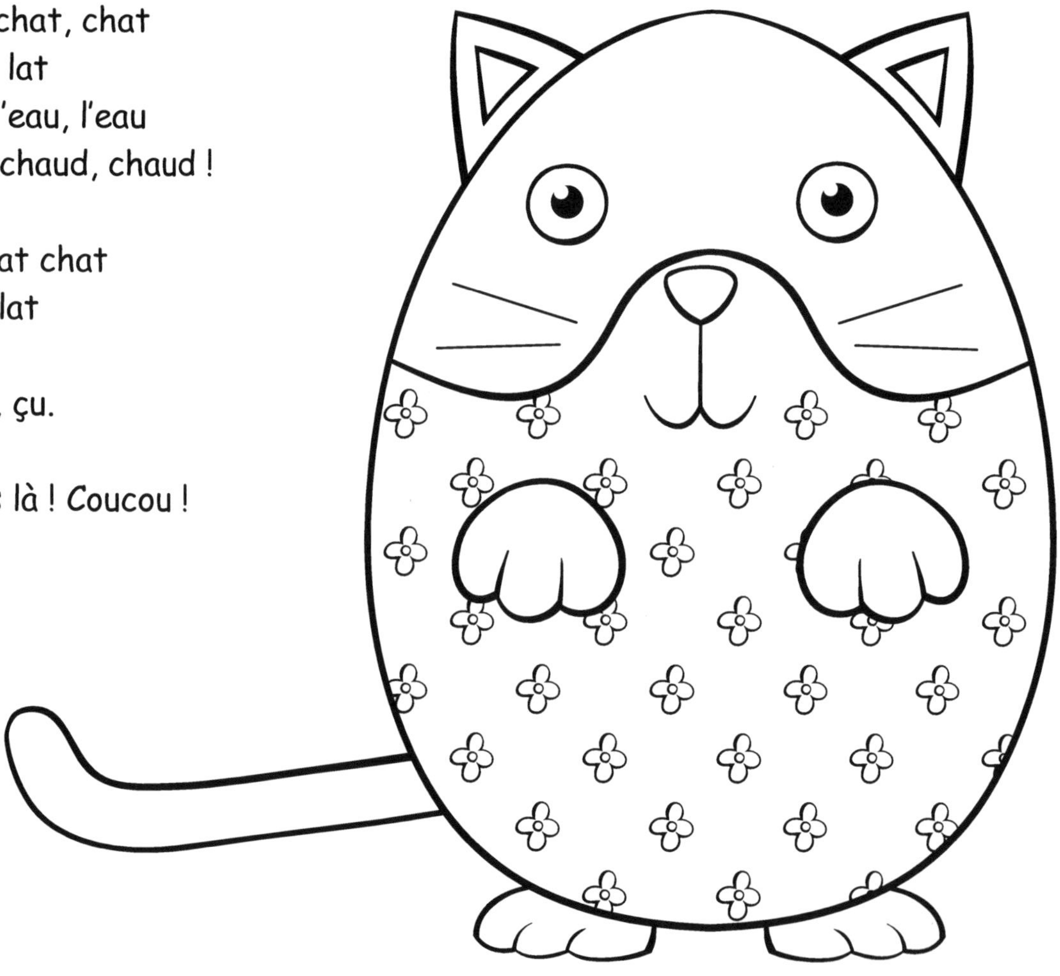

Nom : _____

8. Le chat en chocolat

ch

1. Trace the grapheme below and then practise writing it yourself.

ch   ch   ch

2. Circle the three words below that rhyme with **chat**.

fromage   pas   maison   lundi   rat   œufs   chocolat

3. Circle the word below that means 'happy' in French.

vois   mange   oeufs   heureux   chat   chasser

4. How do we know that the chocolate cat is friendly? Circle the correct answer.

he wags his tail   he smiles   he purrs   he leaves presents

5. What does the chocolate cat drink when he is too hot? Circle the correct answer.

milk   hot chocolate   water   lemonade   tea

5. Which word describes how we feel when the chocolate cat disappears?

fâché   soulagé   déçu   heureux   fatigué   agacé

6. Draw pictures to illustrate the following lines from the song:

Il mange des œufs.	Il me sourit.	Il a trop chaud.

21 Fun Songs to Teach French Phonics   29
© Brilliant Publications Limited   This page may be copied for use by the purchasing institution only.

9. Il y a une petite bête

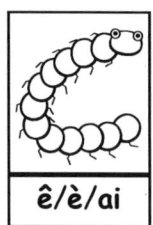

Il y a une petite bête
Qui fait la fête
Sur ma tête !
Il y a une petite bête
Qui fait la fête
Sur ma tête !

Elle danse, elle chante
À tue-tête !
Elle saute, elle crie
À tue-tête !
Il faudrait pas qu'elle pète !

Il y a une petite bête
Qui fait la fête
Sur ma tête !
Il y a une petite bête
Qui fait la fête
Sur ma tête !

Elle danse, elle chante
À tue-tête !
Elle saute, elle crie
À tue-tête !
Il faudrait pas qu'elle pète !

Nom : _____

9. Il y a une petite bête

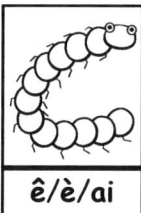
ê/è/ai

1. Trace the graphemes below and then practise writing them yourself. Pay special attention to the accents.

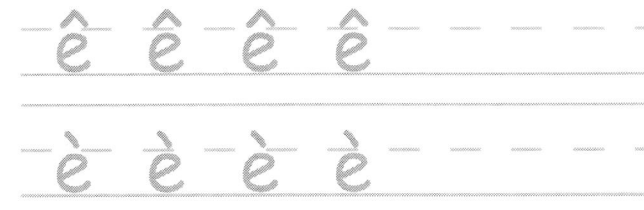

2. Circle the six words below that contain the grapheme **ê**.

rêve   revue   même   maison   être   forêt   feuille   crêpe   cheval   fenêtre

3. Find and colour in the four mini beasts below that contain the grapheme **è**.

4. Draw pictures of the **petite bête** to illustrate the phrases below.

elle chante

elle danse

elle saute

Top tip!
You can also make the same phonic sound using the grapheme **ei**:

beignet      seize   16   neige

21 Fun Songs to Teach French Phonics

10. Petit enfant

an/en/am/em

Petit enfant
Aime sa maman
Et lui demande un jour :

Maman, maman
Quand serai-je grand ?
Je suis petit depuis si longtemps !

Petite maman
Aime son enfant
Et lui réponds toujours :

Ne t'inquiète pas, mon petit chat
Tu seras grand un jour, tu verras !
Mais d'ici là, reste comme ça
Je t'aimerai toujours.

Petit ou grand
Je t'aime autant
C'est pour la vie notre amour
C'est pour la vie notre amour.

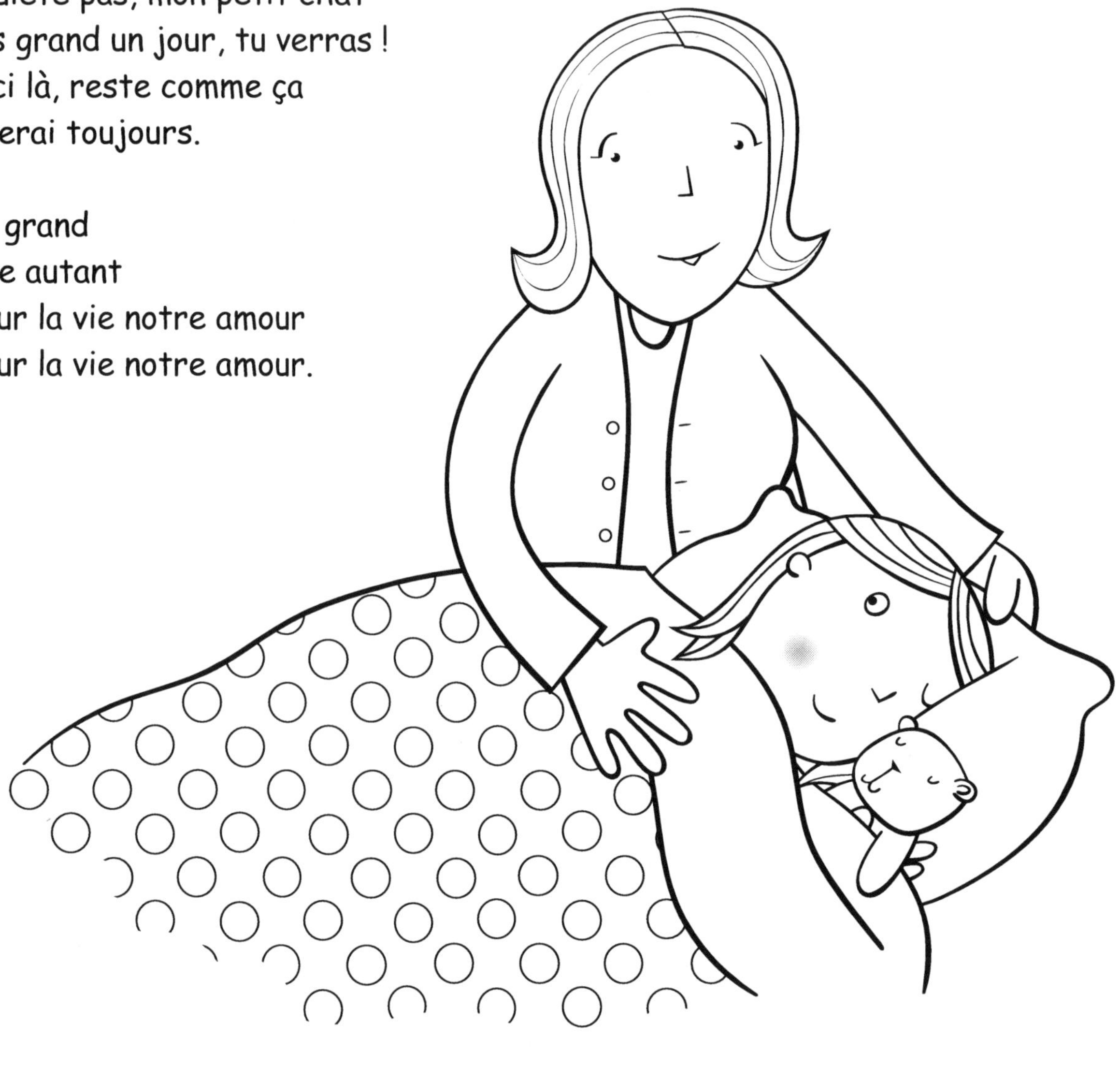

Nom : _____

10. Petit enfant

an/en/am/em

1. Trace the graphemes below then practise writing them yourself.

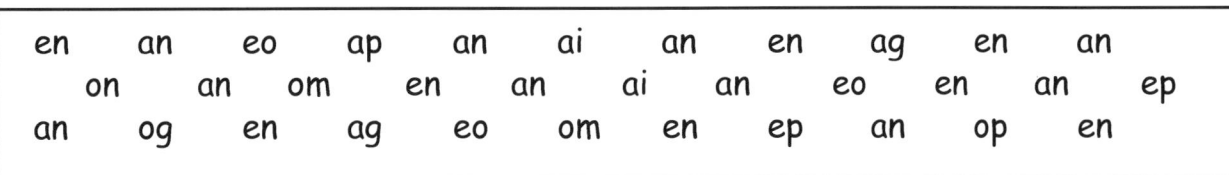

2. Draw a circle around every **en** grapheme and a square around every **an** grapheme.

en	an	eo	ap	an	ai	an	en	ag	en	an
on	an	om	en	an	ai	an	eo	en	an	ep
an	og	en	ag	eo	om	en	ep	an	op	en

How many circles did you draw? ☐   How many squares did you draw? ☐

3. Practise saying the phrases below. Get your partner or teacher to check your pronunciation and colour in the pictures when you are confident you can say all the words correctly.

Petit	Petite
Petit enfant	Petite maman
Petit enfant aime	Petite maman aime
Petit enfant aime sa	Petite maman aime son
Petit enfant aime sa maman	Petite maman aime son enfant

4. Draw a picture of your **maman** in the heart and then write a sentence about her. You can use words from the vocabulary box to help you.

_____

_____

Vocabulary
Ma m**am**an est — My mum is
g**en**tille — kind
marr**an**te — funny
f**an**tastique — fantastic
élég**an**te — elegant

21 Fun Songs to Teach French Phonics
© Brilliant Publications Limited

11. François le serpent

ç/s/ss

François le serpent n'est pas, n'est pas très content !
Il veut faire comme les garçons
Et s'habiller en caleçon
Mais comme il n'a pas de jambes
Chaque fois qu'il essaye, le caleçon tombe, tombe, tombe, tombe !

Ssssssss serpent !

François le serpent, n'est pas, n'est pas très content !
Il veut faire comme les garçons
Et s'habiller en caleçon
Mais comme il n'a pas de jambes
Chaque fois qu'il essaye, le caleçon tombe, tombe, tombe, tombe !

Ssssssss serpent !

Nom : _____

11. François le serpent

ç/s/ss

1. Trace the grapheme below and then practise writing it yourself. Pay special attention to the cedilla accent underneath the letter **c**.

2. Colour in the snakes below that contain the grapheme **ç** (with a cedilla accent).

3. Unscramble the letters below to make the French words for each of the images.

p r e s t n e _____

r a g n o ç _____

n o c e l a ç _____

4. Dress up François using items of clothing and accessories from the vocabulary box. Label your picture.

Vocabulary	
un chapeau	a hat
une écharpe	a scarf
une jupe	skirt
un noeud papillon	a bow tie
un pyjama	pyjamas
une robe	a dress
un sac à main	a handbag
des chaussettes	socks
des chaussures	shoes

5. The French verb for 'to wear' is **porter**. Finish off the sentence below about what François is wearing. The French word for 'and' is **et**.

François porte _____

_____

21 Fun Songs to Teach French Phonics
© Brilliant Publications Limited

12. Gaston le gorille

Tracks 12 & 33

ga, go, gu

Gaston le gorille aime jouer de la guitare
Il n'est jamais fatigué, c'est un vrai fêtard !
Il joue pour ses amis tous les samedis soir
Avec ses godasses dorées, c'est une superstar !

G, g, g, g, g, Gaston ! G, g, g, g, g, gorille ! G, g, g, g, g, guitare !

Gaston le gorille aime jouer de la guitare
Il n'est jamais fatigué, c'est un vrai fêtard !
Il joue pour ses amis tous les samedis soir
Avec ses godasses dorées, c'est une superstar !

G, g, g, g, g, Gaston ! G, g, g, g, g, gorille ! G, g, g, g, g, guitare !

C'est une vraie superstar, oui !

Nom : _____

12. Gaston le gorille

ga, go, gu

1. Trace the graphemes below and then practise writing them yourself.

ga   ga   ga

go   go   go

gu   gu   gu

2. Circle and shade the words below that contain the graphemes **ga**, **go** and **gu**.

garçon	géographie	géant
guerre		goûter
gomme		jaune
girafe		gagner

3. Draw lines to match up the images with the words.

goûter

guitare

godasse

gorille

4. Draw a picture of **Gaston le gorille**.

5. Practise saying out loud: **Gaston le gorille aime jouer de la guitare.** Ask your teacher or a partner to listen to you and then put a tick in the box when you are confident you can say all the words correctly. ☐

Top tip!
In French, the letter 'g' before 'e', 'i' and 'y' is sounded like the 'j' in the word 'bonjour'.

genou   girafe   gymnastique

21 Fun Songs to Teach French Phonics
© Brilliant Publications Limited

13. Gigi et Georges

Gigi la girafe et Georges le rouge-gorge
Sont de très bons amis,
Gigi est aussi grande qu'une géante
Et Georges est tout petit.

Gigi et Georges, Gigi et Georges
Gigi et Georges sont amis.

Un jour Georges demande à Gigi :
Pourquoi ton cou est-il si long ?
Gigi réfléchit et répond :
Car mes pieds ne sentent pas très bon !

Gigi et Georges, Gigi et Georges
Gigi et Georges sont amis.

Georges fait une pause et puis il dit :
Il n'y a pas de soucis
À ma hauteur, j'adore l'odeur
Tes pieds sentent bon les fleurs !

Gigi et Georges, Gigi et Georges
Gigi et Georges sont amis.

Gigi et Georges, Gigi et Georges
Gigi et Georges sont amis.

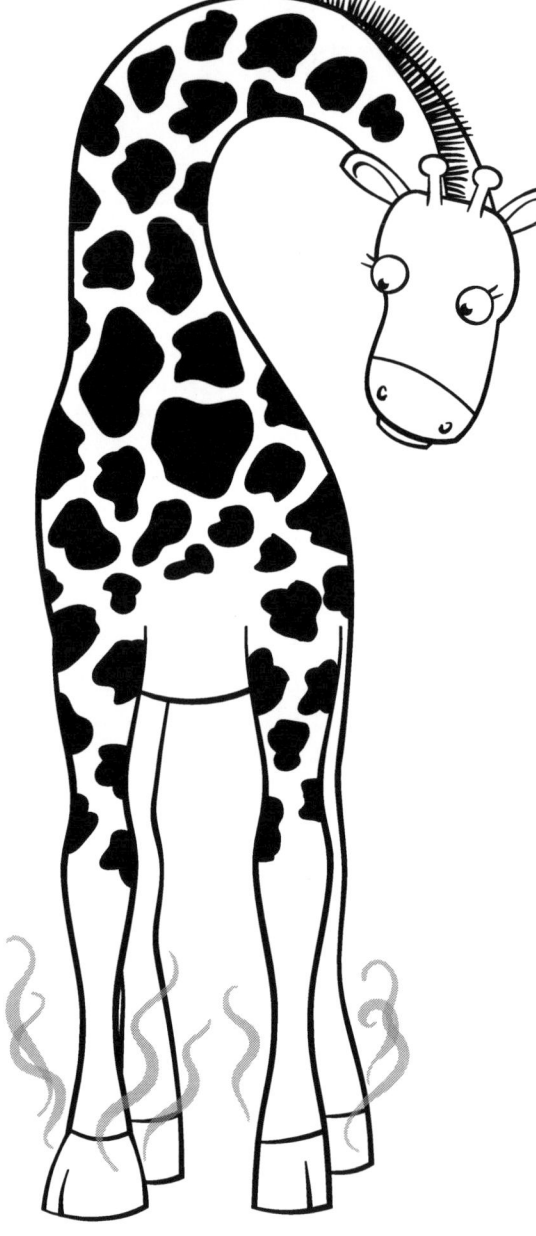

Nom : _____

13. Gigi et Georges

gi, ge

1. Trace the graphemes below and then practise writing them yourself.

gi gi gi gi

ge ge ge ge

2. Draw lines to match up the words on the left with their opposites on the right. You may need to use a dictionary to help you.

grand   vide

froid   vieux

rapide   petit

jeune   chaud

plein   lent

3. Draw a picture of your best friend. Then, using the vocabulary box, write a sentence about why you like him/her.

Vocabulary
J'aime	I like
mon copain	my friend (boy)
ma copine	my friend (girl)
parce qu'il	because he
parce qu'elle	because she
est	is
gentil / gentille	kind (boy/girl)
marrant / marrante	funny (boy/girl)
intelligent / intelligente	clever (boy/girl)
intéressant / intéressante	interesting (boy/girl)

Top tip!
Before the letters 'a', 'o' and 'u', the letter 'g' is pronounced 'hard' like in the English word 'gate'.
    gagner (*to win*)
    gomme (*rubber*)
    guerre (*war*)

14. Chloé et Barnabé

é/et/er

La petite fée Chloé et son ami Barnabé, l'éléphant, l'éléphant,
Ils ne veulent pas aller à l'école en vélo, c'est trop lent, c'est trop lent.
Ils préféreraient y aller en fusée, c'est plus marrant, c'est plus marrant,
Mais comme il y a du vent, ils décident d'y aller en marchant.

La petite fée Chloé et son ami Barnabé, l'éléphant, l'éléphant,
Ils ne veulent pas aller à l'école en vélo, c'est trop lent, c'est trop lent.
Ils préféreraient y aller en fusée, c'est plus marrant, c'est plus marrant,
Mais comme il y a du vent, ils décident d'y aller en sautant.

La petite fée Chloé et son ami Barnabé, l'éléphant, l'éléphant,
Ils ne veulent pas aller à l'école en vélo, c'est trop lent, c'est trop lent.
Ils préféreraient y aller en fusée, c'est plus marrant, c'est plus marrant,
Mais comme il y a du vent, ils décident d'y aller en dansant.

Nom : _____

14. Chloé et Barnabé

é/et/er

1. Trace the graphemes below and then practise writing them yourself. Pay special attention to the acute accent on the letter **e**.

é é é é

et et et et

er er er er

2. Circle all the words that contain the grapheme **é**.

> ami   éléphant   vent   école   fée   lent   fusée   marrant   vélo   petite

How many words did you circle? ☐

3. Practise saying the following French verbs, paying careful attention to the **er** phonic sound at the end. Ask your partner or teacher to listen to your pronunciation and colour in each star when you are confident you can say the verb correctly.

⟨ aller ⟩ ⟨ manger ⟩ ⟨ écouter ⟩ ⟨ regarder ⟩ ⟨ parler ⟩ ⟨ marcher ⟩

4. Which methods of transport would you like to take to go to school? Draw a picture and complete the sentence, using the vocabulary box to help you.

Je voudrais aller à l'école _____

_____

_____

Vocabulary
en voiture 🚗   et (*and*)   en avion ✈️
en bateau ⛵   en hélicoptère 🚁
en train 🚂   ou (*or*)   en montgolfière 🎈

Top tip!
You can also make the same phonic sound using the following spellings:
ez   le n**ez** (*the nose*), tais**ez**-vous (*be quiet*)
es   l**es** (*the*), d**es** (*some*), m**es** (*my*), c**es** (*these*)

21 Fun Songs to Teach French Phonics
© Brilliant Publications Limited

15. Du lundi au dimanche

Voici les jours de la semaine !

Lundi, je reste au lit
Mardi, je mange du riz
Mercredi, je fais du ski
Jeudi, je jongle avec des fruits
Oui, oui, oui, oui !
Vendredi, je dis merci
Samedi, je vois mes amis

Mais le dimanche est différent
Car le « di » est placé à l'avant
Dimanche, dimanche, dimanche !

Et puis c'est lundi et tout recommence !

Lundi, je reste au lit
Mardi, je mange du riz
Mercredi, je fais du ski
Jeudi, je jongle avec des fruits
Oui, oui, oui, oui !
Vendredi, je dis merci
Samedi, je vois mes amis

Mais le dimanche est différent
Car le « di » est placé à l'avant
Dimanche, dimanche, dimanche !

Et puis c'est lundi et tout recommence !

Nom : _____

15. Du lundi au dimanche

i

1. Trace the grapheme below then practise writing it yourself:

i i i i _____

2. Write the French days of the week in the correct order in box A.
Use box B to help you.

A
| _____ d i |
| _____ d i |
| _____ d i |
| _____ d i |
| _____ d i |
| _____ d i |
| d i _____ |

B
| mercre |
| vendre |
| mar |
| lun |
| manche |
| jeu |
| same |

3. Fill in the gaps in each sentence below using the words in the box to help you.

a) Lundi, je reste au _____

b) Mardi, je _____ du riz

c) Mercredi, je fais du _____

d) Jeudi, je jongle avec des _____

e) Vendredi, je dis _____

f) Samedi, je _____ mes amis

| merci |
| ski |
| fruits |
| mange |
| vois |
| lit |

4. Answer the following question in French: **qu'est-ce que tu fais le dimanche ?**
(What do you do on Sundays?) Start your answer with: **Le dimanche, je ….**

_____

_____

Top tip!
Unlike in English, the days of the week in French **do not have capital letters** (unless they are at the start of a sentence).

21 Fun Songs to Teach French Phonics
© Brilliant Publications Limited
This page may be copied for use by the purchasing institution only.

16. Papy, raconte-moi une histoire !

Tracks 16 & 37

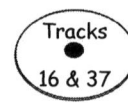

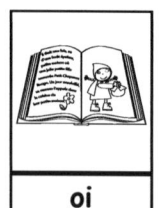

oi

Papy, raconte-moi une histoire !
La nuit, il fait froid et j'ai peur du noir !
Je crois qu'il y a un monstre dans le couloir !
Papy, raconte-moi une histoire !

Une histoire de dragons et de rois
Une histoire de gros loup dans le bois
Une histoire de sheriff qui fait la loi
Une histoire qui raconte n'importe quoi !

Papy, raconte-moi une histoire !
La nuit, il fait froid et j'ai peur du noir !
Je crois qu'il y a un monstre dans le couloir !
Papy, raconte-moi une histoire !

Mon petit coeur, maintenant c'est l'heure
De hisser la grand-voile, à la belle étoile
Laisse-toi bercer et fais dodo
Aux pays des réglisses et chamallows.

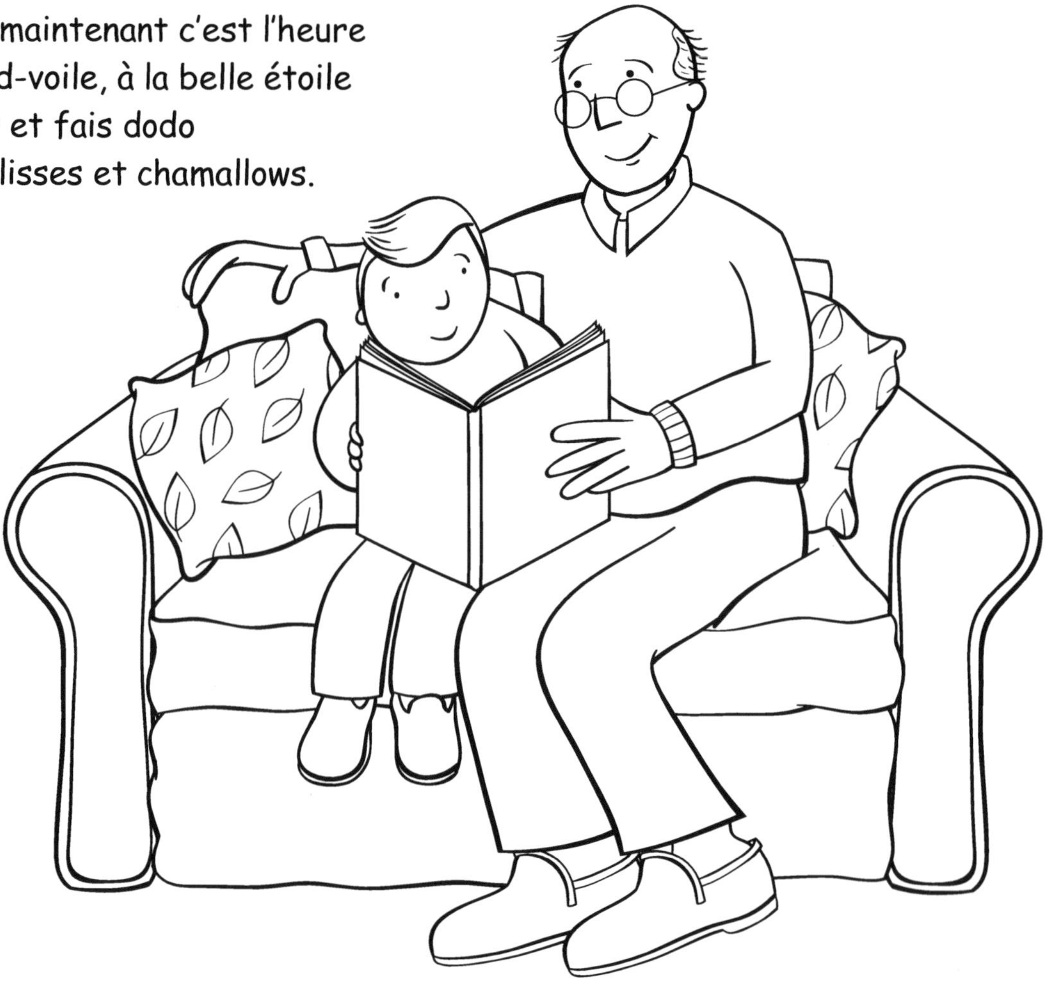

Nom : _____

16. Papy, raconte-moi une histoire !

oi

1. Trace the grapheme below and then practise writing it yourself.

2. Colour in the dragons below that contain the grapheme **oi**.

histoire — froid — monstre — noir — loup — moi

3. Draw pictures to illustrate the following phrases:

Une histoire de dragons et de rois	Une histoire de gros loup dans le bois	Une histoire de sheriff qui fait la loi

4. Complete the crossword below by translating the clues into French.

Across
2 star
4 black
6 hallway

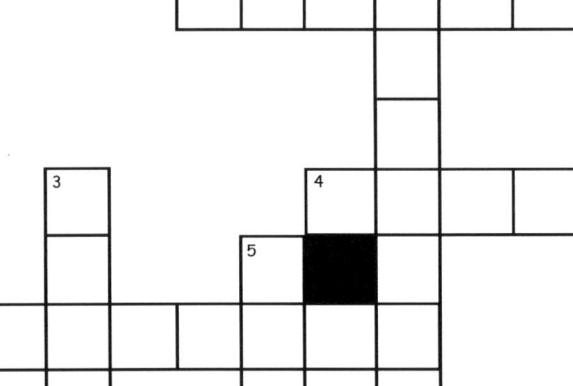

Down
1 story
3 cold
5 king

21 Fun Songs to Teach French Phonics
© Brilliant Publications Limited
45
This page may be copied for use by the purchasing institution only.

17. Une glace à la vanille

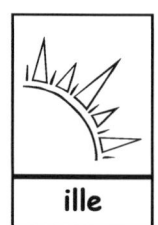

J'aime aller à la plage avec ma famille
J'aime jouer avec tous les garçons et les filles
J'aime sentir sur ma peau le soleil qui brille
Et j'adore manger une glace à la vanille !

Avec une sauce au caramel ! Avec une sauce au caramel !
Avec une sauce au caramel ! Avec une sauce au caramel !

J'aime aller à la plage avec ma famille
J'aime jouer avec tous les garçons et les filles
J'aime sentir sur ma peau le soleil qui brille
Et j'adore manger une glace à la vanille !

Avec une sauce au chocolat ! Avec une sauce au chocolat !
Avec une sauce au chocolat ! Avec une sauce au chocolat !

Nom : _____

17. Une glace à la vanille

ille

1. Trace the grapheme below and then practise writing it yourself.

ille   ille   ille   _____

2. Circle the four words below that contain the grapheme **ille**.

fille   bulle   bille   utile   gorille   sourcils   cheville   milieu   aller

3. Use the images to help you unscramble the words below that contain the grapheme **ille**. You may need a dictionary to help you.

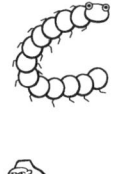    i h n e l c l e   _____

                o q l l i j n u e   _____

   r o l l i g e   _____

                l i f m a l e   _____

4. Colour in the ice creams below according to the description of their flavours.

une glace à la menthe   une glace au citron   une glace à la fraise   une glace au chocolat

5. Using words from the song and/or a dictionary to help you, draw and label in French a picture of you and your **famille à la plage**.

18. Le rap du hérisson

Hervé le hérisson
A mangé trop de bonbons.
Hic hic hic ! Il a le hoquet !
À l'hôpital ! Il faut le soigner !
On y va en hélicoptère
Aïe, aïe, aïe ! Pauvre pépère !

Hector le hippo
A mangé trop de chamallows.
Hic hic hic ! Il a le hoquet !
À l'hôpital ! Il faut le soigner !
On y va en hélicoptère
Aïe, aïe, aïe ! Pauvre pépère !

Harry le hamster
A mangé trop de hamburgers.
Hic hic hic ! Il a le hoquet !
À l'hôpital ! Il faut le soigner !
On y va en hélicoptère
Aïe, aïe, aïe ! Pauvre pépère !

Quelle est la morale de cette histoire ?
Écoute-moi bien et tu vas savoir !
Si tu veux rester en bonne santé
Il faut manger équilibré !
Si tu as compris, chante avec moi :
Hip Hip Hip Hoorah !

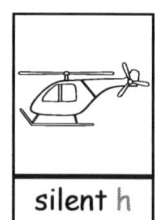

silent h

Nom : _____

18. Le rap du hérisson

Top tip! The letter h is always silent in French.

silent h

1. Practise saying the words below, being careful not to pronounce the letter **h** at the start. Colour in the pictures when you are confident you can say the words correctly.

 hérisson    hélicoptère    hôpital

2. Make up your own story about a greedy animal! Using the vocabulary box below, choose and shade an option from each of the tables, then draw a picture.

a)

Henri		requin		chocolat
Hugo	le	serpent	à mangé trop de	beignets
Hubert		tigre		frites

b)

	mal au ventre !		en moto
Il a	mal à la tête !	À l'hôpital ! On y va	en voiture
	mal à la gorge !		en avion

3. Write out the two French sentences you created in exercise 2.

Vocabulary
- requin — shark
- serpent — snake
- tigre — tiger
- chocolat — chocolate
- beignets — doughnuts
- frites — chips
- mal au ventre — a tummy ache
- mal à la tête — a headache
- mal à la gorge — a sore throat
- en moto — by bike
- en voiture — by car
- en avion — by aeroplane

a) _____

_____

_____

b) _____

_____

_____

4. Practise saying this tongue-twister. Remember not to pronounce the letter **h** !

> Hervé le hérisson a hâte de hiberner cet hiver avec Harry le hamster.

19. Qu'est-ce que ... ?

Qu'est-ce que tu fais aujourd'hui ?
Je joue au foot avec mes amis.

Qu'est-ce que tu as fait hier ?
J'ai fait du skate avec mon frère.

Qu'est-ce que tu vas faire demain ?
Je vais promener mon chien.

Que, que, que, que, qu'est-ce que ?
Que, que, que, que, qu'est-ce que ?
Que, que, que, que, qu'est-ce que ?

Que, que, que, que, qu'est-ce que ?
Que, que, que, que, qu'est-ce que ?
Que, que, que, que, qu'est-ce que ?

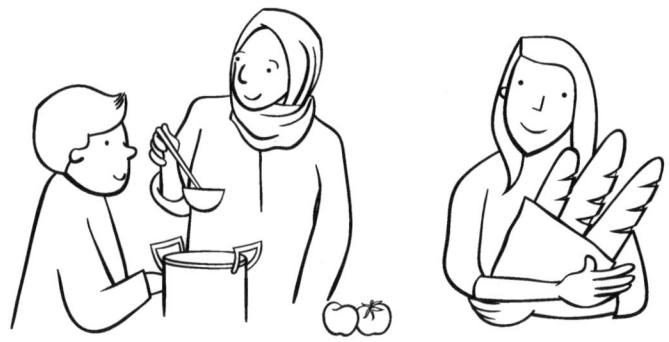

Qu'est-ce que tu fais aujourd'hui ?
Je fais du ski avec mes amis.

Qu'est-ce que tu as fait hier ?
J'ai cuisiné avec ma mère.

Qu'est-ce que tu vas faire demain ?
Je vais acheter du pain.

Que, que, que, que, qu'est-ce que ?
Que, que, que, que, qu'est-ce que ?
Que, que, que, que, qu'est-ce que ?

Que, que, que, que, qu'est-ce que ?
Que, que, que, que, qu'est-ce que ?
Que, que, que, que, qu'est-ce que ?

Qu'est-ce que ?

Nom : _____

19. Qu'est-ce que … ?

qu

1. Trace the grapheme below and then practise writing it yourself:

qu   qu   qu

2. Draw lines to match up the French question words on the left with their English translations on the right. You may need to use a dictionary to help you.

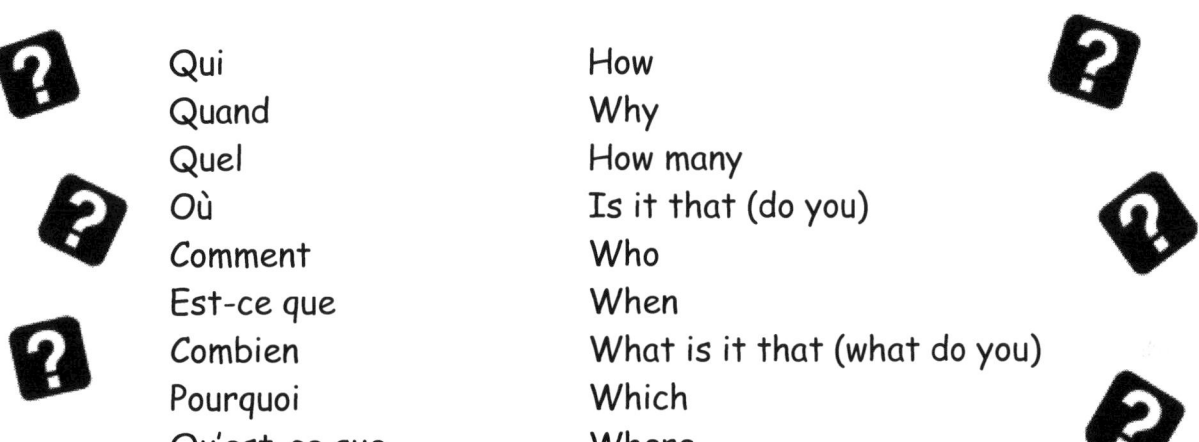

Qui	How
Quand	Why
Quel	How many
Où	Is it that (do you)
Comment	Who
Est-ce que	When
Combien	What is it that (what do you)
Pourquoi	Which
Qu'est-ce que	Where

3. Draw pictures to illustrate the phrases in the boxes below:

Aujourd'hui	Hier	Demain
Je joue au foot avec mes amis.	**J'ai fait** du skate avec mon frère.	**Je vais** promener mon chien.

4. Using the sentence structures in exercise 3 above, write three sentences in French about what you are doing today, what you did yesterday and what you are going to do tomorrow.

Aujourd'hui, je joue _____

Hier, j'ai fait _____

Demain, je vais _____

20. Trois oiseaux

s sounds like z

Il y a trois oiseaux dans mon jardin
Un mange les fraises, un autre les raisins
Le troisième préfère les cerises
Et pour dire merci, il me fait la bise !

Chantez, petits oiseaux
Volez, vous êtes si beaux !
Prenez-moi sous vos ailes
Emmenez-moi dans le ciel.

Il y a trois oiseaux dans mon jardin
Un mange les fraises, un autre les raisins
Le troisième préfère les cerises
Et pour dire merci, il me fait la bise !

Chantez, petits oiseaux !
Volez, vous êtes si beaux !
Prenez-moi sous vos ailes
Emmenez-moi dans le ciel.

Nom : _____

20. Trois oiseaux

s sounds like z

1. In French, the letter **s** sounds like a **z** when it is between two vowels within a word. For example: oi**s**eau, frai**s**e, ceri**s**e, rai**s**in.

   Practise saying the word **oiseau**, paying careful attention to the **z** sound in the middle. Get your partner or teacher to check your pronunciation and colour in a bird each time you say **oiseau** correctly.

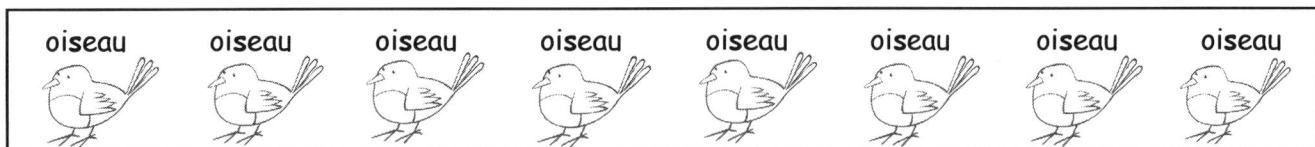

2. An **s** at the end of a word is usually silent. For example: **trois**. However, it is sounded like a **z** when it is followed by a vowel or silent **h** at the start of the next word. This is called a liaison. For example:

trois araignées	trois oiseaux	trois hirondelles
z	z	z

   Practise saying the phrase **trois oiseaux**, paying careful attention to the two **z** sounds. Get your partner or teacher to check your pronunciation and colour in a group of three birds each time you say **trois oiseaux** correctly.

3. Read the description of a garden then draw a picture of it in the box.
   Dans mon jardin, il y a trois arbres et beaucoup de fleurs. Il y a un escargot, deux araignées et trois oiseaux. Il y a aussi quatre fraises, cinq raisins et six cerises.

4. Write a sentence about your ideal garden starting with:
   Dans mon jardin, il y a _____

_____

21 Fun Songs to Teach French Phonics
© Brilliant Publications Limited
This page may be copied for use by the purchasing institution only.

21. Le petit canard Coin-coin

oin

Le petit canard Coin-coin
Un jour est parti trop loin
Il s'est perdu dans le foin
Il a besoin d'un coup de main.

Allez, Coin-coin
Ne vas pas trop loin
Allez, Coin-coin
Viens voir tes copains
Allez Coin-coin, Coin-coin.

Le petit canard Coin-coin,
Un jour est parti trop loin
Il s'est perdu dans le foin
Il a besoin d'un coup de main.

Allez, Coin-coin
Ne vas pas trop loin
Allez, Coin-coin
Viens voir tes copains
C'est l'heure de prendre ton bain.

Coin-coin !

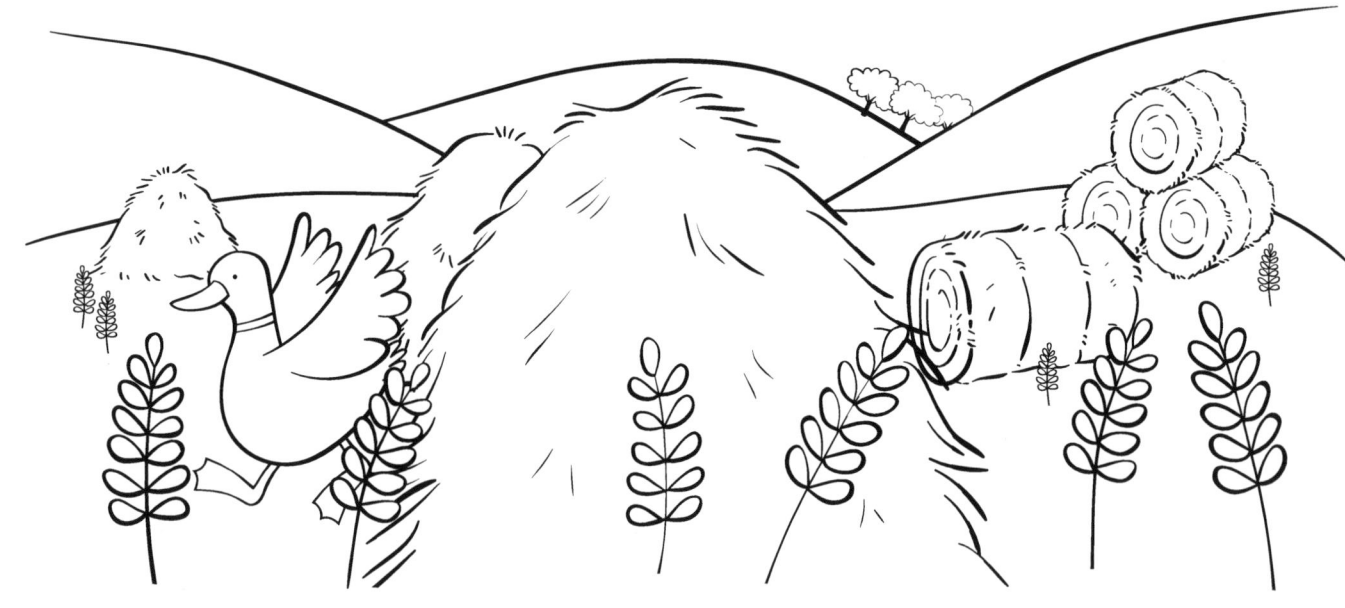

Nom : _____

21. Le petit canard Coin-coin

oin

1. Trace the grapheme below and then practise writing it yourself:

oin   oin   oin

2. Circle the four words below that contain the grapheme **oin**.

> poids   loin   fois   coin   grenouille   besoin   témoin   toît

3. Complete the word search below, then translate the words into English. The words can go forwards, backwards, up and down and diagonally.

```
o c v z t c a k o z i h a f t
o b t r y a z r d f d y l m f
k r n j o n q n f m w y x e h
f b l y c a a n e i h c r c o
h u n q e r o k z g q l p g n
m v x i g d x t m t i t e p e
w d e l o m a v t t g u j g w
m w o c w s h m b t z u l x n
n a l j v b e q p d e i d s q
z c h e v a l b e m r e f e i
q n i o f w c z n o h c o c r
p q o t k l s h w i h d s c b
j x t o e v p t g h o v b u t
s y o j x i q z v i a l s q n
b u n e q x j s n k g n p r r
```

canard _____

cheval _____

chien _____

foin _____

loin _____

besoin _____

cochon _____

petit _____

grand _____

ferme _____

4. Colour in the picture below according to the following colour code:

Coin-coin = jaune
foin = marron
cochon = rose
chien = noir
cheval = gris

21 Fun Songs to Teach French Phonics
© Brilliant Publications Limited
This page may be copied for use by the purchasing institution only.

French phonics progress chart

Key graphemes

Colour in each picture as you learn its phonic sound.

un 
un

o cachalot	**ou** loup	**gn** araignée	**u** tortue
on cochon	**ien** chien	**ch** chat	**ê** bête
en/an enfant	**ç** caleçon	**go** gorille	**gi** girafe
é éléphant	**i** ski	**oi** histoire	**ille** brille
silent h hélicoptère	**qu** qu'est-ce que ?	**s sounds like z** oiseaux	**oin** Coin-coin

French phonics progress chart

All graphemes used in songs

Colour in each picture as you learn its phonic sound.

			un  un
o/eau cachalot	**ou/où** loup	**gn** araignée	**u** tortue
on cochon	**ien** chien	**ch** chat	**ê/è/ai** bête
en/an/em/am enfant	**ç/s/ss** caleçon	**ga/go/gu** gorille	**gi/ge/gé/j** girafe
é/et/er éléphant	**i** ski	**oi** histoire	**ille** brille
silent h hélicoptère	**qu** qu'est-ce que ?	**s sounds like z** oiseaux	**oin** Coin-coin

21 Fun Songs to Teach French Phonics

English translations

1. Il y a quelqu'un ?   page 14
Is anybody there?

Hello, hello!
Is anybody there?

Yes! It's me! Little brown rabbit!

Dance, sing, clap,
Three, two, one
Say hello to little brown rabbit.

Hello, hello!
Is anybody there?

Yes! It's me! Little brown horse!

Dance, sing, clap,
Three, two, one
Say hello to little brown horse.

Hello, hello!
Is anybody there?

Yes! It's me! Little brown bird!

Dance, sing, clap,
Three, two, one
Say hello to little brown bird.

2. Mon cachalot   page 16
My whale

I have a bucket
A lovely bucket
In my bucket
There is some water.

I have a bucket
A lovely bucket
In my bucket
A whale is hiding.

A whale?
A whale!

Wow! How big he is!
Wow! How handsome he is!
My whale
Splash!

3. Mon petit loup   page 18
My little wolf

Where are you, my little wolf,
My little wolf, so soft?

I'm playing in the mud
With my friend, the owl.

Where are you, my little wolf,
My little wolf, so soft?

I'm playing in the mud
With my friend, the owl.

My little wolf
You don't love me anymore!
You're always with your owl!

Don't be silly!
Don't be mad!
Come and party with us,
Come and party with us!

We're having a party?
Great!

4. Une araignée dans ma baignoire   page 20
A spider in my bathtub

There is a spider in my bathtub
It's hairy, big and black all over!
I'm not even scared, no, no, no,
It's cute to have a spider as a friend.

It's cute, cute, cute, cute
It's cute, cute, cute, cute.

There is a spider in my bathtub
It's hairy, big and black all over!
I'm not even scared, no, no, no,
It's cute to have a spider as a friend.

It's cute, cute, cute, cute
It's cute, cute, cute, cute.

What about you? Do you like spiders?

5. Lulu la tortue   page 22
Lulu the turtle

Lulu the turtle
Decided one day
To travel across the universe
In her little rocket.

5, 4, 3, 2, 1 – whoosh!

She had a picnic on the moon
She played football on Neptune
And after this extraordinary journey,
Very gently,
Very gently,
Very gently…
She came back down to Earth
She came back down to Earth.

6. Le rock 'n' rock du cochon   page 24
The piggy rock 'n' roll

Roll up, roll up, we're going to sing the animal rock 'n' roll song!

The animal rock 'n' roll
The animal rock 'n' roll

The pig, the pig, the pig… is eating sweets!

The animal rock 'n' roll
The animal rock 'n' roll

The sheep, the sheep, the sheep… is mowing the lawn!

The animal rock 'n' roll
The animal rock 'n' roll

The lion, the lion, the lion… is playing the violin!

The animal rock 'n' roll
The animal rock 'n' roll

The fish, the fish, the fish… is wearing a pair of trousers!

The animal rock 'n' roll
The animal rock 'n' roll

The hedgehog, the hedgehog, the hedgehog… is flying an aeroplane!

They are so cute!

7. Mon ami Julien   page 26
My friend Julien

I have a friend called Julien
He would like a little dog
But his dad says: no, no, no!

There's no point having a little dog
When you already have a penguin!

I have a friend called Julien
He would like a little dog
But his dad says: no, no, no!

There's no point having a little dog
When you already have a baboon!

I have a friend called Julien
He would like a little dog
But his dad says: no, no, no!

There's no point having a little dog
When you already have a shark!

Rather than a dog, daddy dear,
How about a little brother?

On second thoughts Julien,
A little dog will be fine!

8. Le chat en chocolat page 28
The cat made out of chocolate

I see the cat, cat, cat
Of chocolate, late, late
He doesn't want, want, want
To chase the rat, rat, rat!

I see the cat, cat, cat
Of chocolate, late, late
Eating eggs, eggs, eggs
He is happy, py, py!

I see the cat, cat, cat
Of chocolate, late, late
Smiling at me, me, me
He is my friend, friend, friend!

I see the cat, cat, cat
Of chocolate, late, late
Drinking water, ter, ter
He is too hot, hot, hot!

The little cat, cat, cat
Of chocolate, late, late
Has disappeared, peared, peared,
I'm disappointed, ted, ted.

No, I'm here! Coo-ey!

9. Il y a une petite bête   page 30
There is a little bug

There is a little bug
Having a party
On my head!
There is a little bug
Having a party
On my head!

It's dancing, it's singing
At the top of its voice!
It's jumping, it's shouting
At the top of its voice!
It had better not trump!

There is a little bug
Having a party
On my head!
There is a little bug
Having a party
On my head!

It's dancing, it's singing
At the top of its voice!
It's jumping, it's shouting
At the top of its voice!
It had better not trump!

10. Petit enfant   page 32
Little child

Little child
Loves his mother
And asks her one day:

Mummy, mummy,
When will I be big?
I have been little for such a long time!

Little mother
Loves her child so much
And always replies:
Don't worry, my little cat
You'll be big one day, you'll see!
Until then, stay as you are
I will always love you.

Fun French Phonic Songs
© Brilliant Publications Limited

Little or big
I love you just the same
Our love will last forever
Our love will last forever.

11. François le serpent
page 34

François the snake

François the snake isn't, isn't very happy!
He wants to be like other boys
And dress himself in boxer shorts
But since he doesn't have any legs
Every time he tries, the boxer shorts fall down, down, down, down!

Ssssssss snake!

François the snake isn't, isn't very happy!
He wants to be like other boys
And dress himself in boxer shorts
But since he doesn't have any legs
Every time he tries, the boxer shorts fall down, down, down, down!

Ssssssss snake!

12. Gaston le gorille   page 36
Gaston the gorilla

Gaston the gorilla likes playing the guitar
He is never tired, he's a real party animal!
He plays for his friends every Saturday evening,
With his gold shoes, he's a superstar!

G, g, g, g, g, Gaston! G, g, g, g, g, gorilla! G, g, g, g, g, guitar!

Gaston the gorilla likes playing the guitar
He is never tired, he's a real party animal!
He plays for his friends every Saturday evening,
With his gold shoes, he's a superstar!

G, g, g, g, g, Gaston! G,g, g, g, g, gorilla! G, g, g, g, g, guitar!

He's a real superstar, yeah!

13. Gigi et Georges   page 38
Gigi and George

Gigi the giraffe and George the robin
Are very good friends,
Gigi is as tall as a giant
And George is teeny-tiny.

Gigi and George, Gigi and George
Gigi and George are good friends.

One day George asks Gigi:
Why is your neck so long?
Gigi thinks about it and replies:
Because my feet don't smell very nice!

Gigi and George, Gigi and George
Gigi and George are good friends.

George pauses and then he says:
Don't worry about it
From where I'm standing, I love the odour,
Your feet smell like flowers to me!

Gigi and George, Gigi and George
Gigi and George are good friends

Gigi and George, Gigi and George
Gigi and George are good friends

14. Chloé et Barnabé page 40
Chloe and Barnaby

Chloe, the little fairy, and her friend Barnaby the elephant, the elephant,
Don't want to go to school by bike, it's too long, it's too long.
They would prefer to go by rocket, that's more fun, that's more fun,
But since it's windy, they decide to walk there instead.

Chloe, the little fairy, and her friend Barnaby the elephant, the elephant
Don't want to go to school by bike, it's too long, it's too long.
They would prefer to go by rocket, that's more fun, that's more fun,
But since it's windy, they decide to jump there instead.

Chloe, the little fairy, and her friend Barnaby the elephant, the elephant
Don't want to go to school by bike, it's too long, it's too long.
They would prefer to go by rocket, that's more fun, that's more fun,
But since it's windy, they decide to dance there instead.

15. Du lundi au dimanche
page 42

From Monday to Sunday

Here are the days of the week!

Monday, I stay in bed
Tuesday, I eat rice
Wednesday, I go skiing
Thursday, I juggle with some fruit
Yeah, yeah, yeah, yeah!
Friday, I say thank you
Saturday, I see my friends
But Sunday is different
Because the 'di' is placed at the front
Sunday, Sunday, Sunday!

And then it's Monday and it starts all over again!

Monday, I stay in bed
Tuesday, I eat rice
Wednesday, I go skiing
Thursday, I juggle with some fruit
Yeah, yeah, yeah, yeah!
Friday, I say thank you
Saturday, I see my friends
But Sunday is different
Because the 'di' is placed at the front
Sunday, Sunday, Sunday!

And then it's Monday and it starts all over again!

16. Papy, raconte-moi une histoire! page 44

Grandpa, tell me a story!

Grandpa, tell me a story!
At night, it's cold and I'm afraid of the dark.
I think there's a monster in the hallway!
Grandpa, tell me a story!

A story of dragons and kings
A story of a big wolf in the woods
A story of a sheriff laying down the law
A story about anything at all!

Grandpa, tell me a story!
At night, it's cold and I'm afraid of the dark.
I think there's a monster in the hallway!
Grandpa, tell me a story!
My little sweetheart, now it's time
To set sail under the stars
Let yourself be rocked and go to sleep
In the land of liquorice and marshmallows.

17. Une glace à la vanille
page 46

Vanilla ice cream

I like going to the beach with my family
I like playing with all the boys and girls
I like feeling the sun shining on my skin
And I love eating vanilla ice cream!

With caramel sauce! With caramel sauce!
With caramel sauce! With caramel sauce!

I like going to the beach with my family
I like playing with all the boys and girls
I like feeling the sun shining on my skin
And I love eating vanilla ice cream!

With chocolate sauce! With chocolate sauce!
With chocolate sauce! With chocolate sauce!

18. Le rap du hérisson
page 48

The hedgehog rap

Harvey the hedgehog
Has eaten too many sweets
Hic hic hic! He's got the hiccups!
To hospital! He needs to be treated!
Let's go by helicopter
Ouch, ouch, ouch! Poor thing!

Hector the hippo
Has eaten too many marshmallows
Hic hic hic! He's got the hiccups!
To hospital! He needs to be treated!
Let's go by helicopter
Ouch, ouch, ouch! Poor thing!

Harry the hamster
Has eaten too many hamburgers
Hic hic hic! He's got the hiccups!
To hospital! He needs to be treated!
Let's go by helicopter
Ouch, ouch, ouch! Poor thing!

What is the moral of this story?
Listen carefully and you will find out
If you want to stay fit
You need to eat healthily!
If you've got it, sing with me:
Hip, hip, hip hooray!

19. Qu'est-ce que ... ? page 50
What...?

What are you doing today?
I'm playing football with my friends.

What did you do yesterday?
I went skateboarding with my brother.

What are you going to do tomorrow?
I'm going to walk my dog.

W – w – w -w what?
W – w – w -w what?
W – w – w -w what?

W – w – w -w what?
W – w – w -w what?
W – w – w -w what?

What are you doing today?
I'm going skiing with my friends.
What did you do yesterday?
I cooked with my mum.

What are you going to do tomorrow?
I am going to buy some bread.

W – w – w -w what?
W – w – w -w what?
W – w – w -w what?

W – w – w -w what?
W – w – w -w what?
W – w – w -w what?

What?

20. Trois oiseaux   page 52
Three birds

There are three birds in my garden
One eats strawberries, another eats grapes
The third prefers cherries
And to say thank you, he kisses me on the cheek!

Sing, little birds!
Fly, you are so beautiful!
Take me underneath your wings
Carry me to the sky.

There are three birds in my garden
One eats strawberries, another eats grapes
The third prefers cherries
And to say thank you, he kisses me on the cheek!

Sing, little birds!
Fly, you are so beautiful!
Take me underneath your wings
Carry me to the sky.

21. Le petit canard Coin-coin   page 52
Quack-quack the little duck

Quack-quack the little duck
Went too far one day
He got lost in the hay
He needs a helping hand.

Come on, Quack-quack
Don't go too far
Come on, Quack-quack
Come and see your friends
Come on Quack-quack, Quack-quack.

Quack-quack the little duck
Went too far one day
He got lost in the hay
He needs a helping hand.

Come on, Quack-quack
Don't go too far
Come on, Quack-quack
Come and see your friends
It's time to take your bath!

Quack-quack!

Answers

1. Il y a quelqu'un ?   page 15
2. <u>jun</u>gle = jungle
   <u>lun</u>di = Monday
   br<u>un</u> = brown
   chac<u>un</u> = each one
   <u>un</u> = one/a/an
3. Illustrations of: a little purple rabbit; a little green horse; a little blue bird
4. <u>un</u>   s<u>i</u>x
   d<u>eu</u>x   sept
   tr<u>oi</u>s   h<u>ui</u>t
   quatr<u>e</u>   n<u>eu</u>f
   c<u>i</u>nq   d<u>i</u>x

2. Mon cachalot   page 17
2. **gros** (fat), **stylo** (pen), **dos** (back), **mot** (word)

3. **seau** (bucket), **bateau** (boat), **beau** (beautiful), **chapeau** (hat)

4. **cachalot** (sperm whale)

3. Mon petit loup   page 19
2.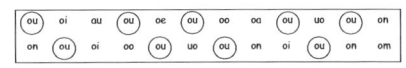

   9
3. l<u>ou</u>p = wolf
   hib<u>ou</u> = owl
   b<u>ou</u>les = boules
   gad<u>ou</u>e = mud
4.

fourmi	souris	journal	tortue
poule	bateau	douche	boîte
amour	bonbon	soupe	route

fourmi (ant), **souris** (mouse), **journal** (newspaper), **poule** (hen), **douche** (shower), **amour** (love), **soupe** (soup), **route** (road)
8

4. Une araignée dans ma baignoire   page 21
2.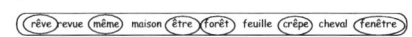

   montagne (mountain), **poignet** (wrist), **mignon** (cute), **baignoire** (bathtub)

5. Lulu la tortue   page 23
None.

6. Le rock 'n' rock du cochon   page 25
2. **cochon** (pig), **mouton** (sheep), **lion** (lion), **poisson** (fish), **hérisson** (hedgehog)
3. **bonbon** = sweet
   gazon = grass lawn
   violon = violin
   pantalon = trousers
   avion = aeroplane
3. Illustrations of: a pig eating sweets; a fish wearing a pair of trousers; a hedgehog piloting an aeroplane.

7. Mon ami Julien   page 27
2.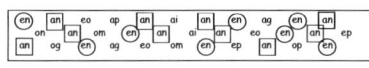

   chien (dog), **rien** (nothing), **bien** (good), **magicien** (magician)
3. Illustrations of: penguin; baboon; shark

8. Le chat en chocolat page 29
1. **pas** (not), **rat** (rat), **chocolat** (chocolate)

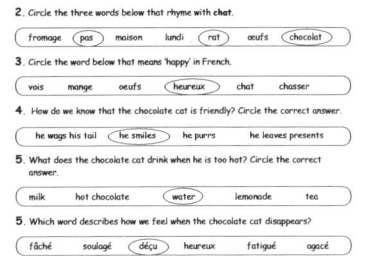

2. **heureux**
3. he smiles
4. water
5. **déçu** (disappointed)
6. Illustrations of: he eats eggs; he is smiling at me; he is too hot.

9. Il y a une petite bête   page 31
2.

   rêve (dream), **même** (same), **être** (to be), **forêt** (forest), **crêpe** (crepe), **fenêtre** (window)
3.
4. Illustrations of bug on the head: singing; dancing; jumping.

10. Petit enfant   page 33
2.

   circles = 8
   squares = 10

11. François le serpent   page 35
2.
3. **serpent** (snake), **garçon** (boy), **caleçon** (boxer shorts)

12. Gaston le gorille   page 36
2.

   garçon (boy), **guerre** (war), **gomme** (rubber), **goûter** (snack), **gagner** (to win)

3. **goûter** = snack
   guitare = guitar
   gorille = gorilla
   godasse = shoe

13. Gigi et Georges   page 39
2. **grand** (big)   **petit** (small)
   froid (cold)   **chaud** (hot)
   rapide (fast) **lent** (slow)
   jeune (young) **vieux** (old)
   plein (full)   **vide** (empty)

14. Chloé et Barnabé   page 41
2.

éléphant (elephant), **école** (school), **fée** (fairy), **fusée** (rocket), **vélo** (bike)
5

15. Du lundi au dimanche   page 43
2. <u>lun</u>**di**
   <u>mar</u>**di**
   <u>mercre</u>**di**
   <u>jeu</u>**di**
   <u>vendre</u>**di**
   <u>same</u>**di**
   di<u>manche</u>

3. a) **lit** (bed), b) **mange** (eat), c) **ski** (skiing), d) **fruits** (fruit), e) **merci** (thank you), f) **vois** (see)

16. Papy, raconte-moi une histoire !   page 45
2.

histoire (story), **froid** (cold), **noir** (black), **moi** (me)

3. Illustrations of stories about: dragons and kings; a big wolf in the woods; a sheriff laying down the law

4.

17. Une glace à la vanille   page 47
2.

(fille) bulle (bille) utile (gorille) sourcils (cheville) milieu aller

fille (girl), **bille** (marble), **gorille** (gorilla), **cheville** (ankle)

3. **chenille** (caterpillar), **jonquille** (daffodil), **gorille** (gorilla), **famille** (family)

4. **menthe** (mint) = green
   citron (lemon) = yellow
   fraise (strawberry) = red
   chocolat (chocolate) = brown

18. Le rap du hérisson   page 49
None.

19. Qu'est-ce que ... ?   page 51
2. **Qui**   = Who
   Quand   = When
   Quel   = Which
   Où   = Where
   Comment   = How
   Est-ce que = Is it that (do you)
   Combien   = How many
   Pourquoi   = Why
   Qu'est-ce que = What is it that (what do you)

3. Illustrations of: I'm playing football with my friends; I went skateboarding with my brother; I am going to walk my dog

20. Trois oiseaux   page 53
2. **trois araignées** = 3 spiders
   trois oiseaux = 3 birds
   trois hirondelles = 3 swallows

3. In my garden, there are three trees and lots of flowers. There is a snail, two spiders and three birds. There are also four strawberries, five grapes and six cherries.

21. Le petit canard Coin-coin   page 55
2.

poids (loin) fois (coin) grenouille (besoin) (témoin) toît

loin (far), **coin** (corner), **besoin** (need), **témoin** (witness)

3.

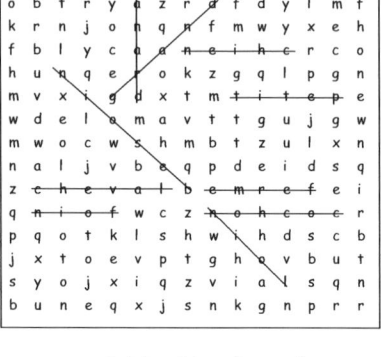

canard (duck), **cheval** (horse), **chien** (dog), **foin** (hay), **loin** (far), **besoin** (need), **cochon** (pig); **petit** (little), **grand** (big), **ferme** (farm)

4. Colour code for illustration:
   Coin-coin (duck) = yellow
   foin (hay) = brown
   cochon (pig) = pink
   chien (dog) = black
   cheval (horse) = grey